· THE ·
DOMESTIC
REVOLUTION
EXPLAINED

THE
DOMESTIC
REVOLUTION
EXPLAINED
FROM BRAINWAVE
TO MICROWAVE

STAN YORKE

COUNTRYSIDE BOOKS
NEWBURY BERKSHIRE

First published 2008
© Stan Yorke 2008

COUNTRYSIDE BOOKS
3 Catherine Road
Newbury, Berkshire

To view our complete range of books,
please visit us at
wwwcountrysidebooks.co.uk

ISBN 978 1 84674 113 5

Designed by Peter Davies, Nautilus Design
Produced through MRM Associates Ltd., Reading

Printed by Information Press, Oxford

CONTENTS

Introduction

Today we all expect water to come out of our taps, the toilet to flush, the lights to go on when we operate the switch and the central heating to burst into life when needed. Yet, less than 150 years ago, most people had no clean running water supply, no flushing toilets and hadn't even dreamt of electric lights or central heating. The modern utility services have become so integrated into our lives that we forget how they all started, even the term 'utilities' sounds boring! As with so many aspects of our lives these advances were achieved through many years of political wrangling, technical developments and enormous disruption, all stirred by the wonderful Victorian enthusiasm for things new.

In this book we follow the story from the 1750s to the 1950s, looking at how our domestic life changed, how health improved and how our homes were revolutionized. Rather than just looking at the social history of the period I have woven the story around the four major utilities which were born of this era, water, sewage, gas and electricity. These industries had their effect on every part of life but here I want to look at how they came into being, how they worked and how they changed the domestic life of the people.

Probably the biggest difficulty for us today is to try and imagine what life was like before this revolution took place. Pre-Victorian society is traditionally looked on as having just two layers, early industrial or rural workers and the landowners, i.e. the poor and the rich! During our story we will see the emergence of that third layer, the middle classes who pioneered so much of what we enjoy today.

As always, money was required in order to benefit from the latest domestic improvements and so we see a time shift between the classes, with the rich inevitably enjoying the new developments first. This shift was often quite immense, being a full 100 years in many cases.

As well as simple costs there was another controlling force on the spread of the utilities – geography. The basic facilities showed an alarming reluctance to spread outside the larger towns and cities. Many villages didn't have mains water until the 1950s and 60s and main sewerage even later. Gas has never reached many areas of the country, though thankfully electricity has made it to almost everyone.

Despite the out-of-sight nature of these subjects there are plenty of museums that feature the utilities and domestic life. A delightful bonus is that many museums recreate the domestic scene, right down to complete houses with burning coal fires and guides in period costume. Indeed most of the pictures and a lot of the information in this book have come from these sites and their ever-helpful staff.

As always in the Living History series I have avoided technical terms wherever possible and the book is packed with pictures and drawings which I hope will help to show how this area of our lives has a fascinating history.

Stan Yorke

To times gone by

NOTE FOR READERS

Throughout the book I have used the units of the period, i.e. feet, gallons and so on. For those of metric persuasion, below is a quick conversion guide.

A foot is approximately 30 cm, a yard is approximately 91.5 cm.
A gallon is approximately 4.5 litres.
A cubic foot is approximately 27 litres.

SECTION
I

1750 – 1850

CHAPTER I

The Simple Life

It doesn't take much imagination to understand why the early use of water was kept to a minimum. All the illustrations I have found invariably show this task being carried out by the women or children of the house.

This period signals the end of a relatively static era which drifts back to the 12th century and during which change was slow and invention, as opposed to development, fairly rare. Life was still predominately rural, with comfortable houses for the landed gentry and little more than hovels for the farm workers. The main cities were long established, almost always on well-organized rivers or estuaries, where the centre of administration or the church sat uncomfortably next to water-borne commerce. Towns, being smaller, had a more gentle and compact feel and were invariably associated with local industry or agriculture. Villages as we think of them today were virtually non-existent. There was a simple reason for this structure – transport, or rather the lack of it. People collected together to form self-contained groups, within which were representatives of all the vital skills needed for life – the farmer for food, builders and carpenters for the houses, the blacksmith for ironware and implements, the candle maker for lighting, the apothecary who was also the doctor. Timber for most uses would be grown locally and any materials, like iron, that were not local had to be carted from larger cities where river or sea provided the long-distance transport. Stone would be used in building if a local quarry existed, and if suitable clay were found in the area a small brickworks would serve the town. A church would tend the soul and the local inn or alehouse the body. Work revolved around these activities with the absolute minimum of travel. We must bear in mind that many of our present-day villages were once small towns with perhaps five or six shops and several rural workshops, all made redundant by the motor car. This need to be self-contained set a minimum size for a town to be viable.

This list of physical necessities, however, leaves out one vital ingredient – water to drink, cook and wash. This was taken from rivers, wells or bore holes. In most towns it was collected from a pump positioned over a well or from a local river or stream and it had to be carried home, a task that quickly made one very frugal in its use. Water was reused whenever possible and eventually went onto the vegetable patch. The old image of Dad bathing in an iron tub in front of a wood-burning fire on a Friday is

Enterprising water carriers would fill their barrels, hopefully from a clean source, and then sell the water in the more affluent parts of town.

Stone-built privy at the bottom of the garden. The wooden seat would hinge up to allow the bucket to be removed for dumping. If one was lucky, there might be a heap of soil and ash with a shovel to help keep down the smell. (Ironbridge – Blists Hill Victorian Town)

provide a small quantity of loose soil which was thrown over the contents. When the ditch was full a new one would be dug and the privy moved over, with some of the soil from the new dig used to cover the previous one. If wood was burnt for heat and cooking, then the ash would be added to the soil as the charcoal and carbon dust was more efficient at keeping the smell down. In time nature did its work and the soil became usable again. For those without the use of a privy, a bucket would be used, the contents being simply thrown into the nearest ditch – rain and time being left to do the best they could. This method, alas, was also used in the larger towns where the closeness of the houses precluded any private garden. It can seem strange to us today to find that water and sewerage started life as completely separate industries and that except for a series of unfortunate events we might not have had a sewerage system until much later.

I started this chapter with comments on the end of an era, and by 1800 the start of a new vastly different world was already under way. The Industrial Revolution was the result of the meeting of many inventions and discoveries. The canals had provided the first means of moving vast quantities of coal, and steam engines had developed from lumbering giants into reliable workhorses. Key to many of the domestic changes was the factory where a product was mass-produced and then sent far afield to be sold. Factories depended on full-time workers, people who would have no time to grow their food or tend the land; these people needed to be able to buy their food. Though this sounds

quite true but what isn't so often mentioned is that Mum used the same water next, followed by the children. Today it might do us well to remember that, though we need around seven pints of water a day to live, we currently each use over 33 gallons every day!

The other requirement was to dispose of sewage. In its most basic form this would be a simple privy, just a small square hut with a plank for sitting on. Dad would dig a ditch over which the privy would stand and

Cast-iron access door for the night soil men to reach the privy bucket. (North of England Open Air Museum)

completely natural to us today, it was the start of a massive social change in the early 1800s.

In larger towns and cities the provision of both water and sewage disposal became more and more problematical. With less private land in which sewage could be buried, more and more waste went into the ditches and streets or straight into the rivers and streams. In many towns privies were built at the bottom of the

garden, with the bucket accessible from outside the rear wall through a door. At night the buckets would be removed and emptied by the night soil men and the resultant collected waste would be dumped well away from housing, or sometimes even sold as fertilizer.

The official method of treating sewage was to dig a cesspit into which the sewage discharged, possibly via a simple pipe system if one was rich.

In Manchester just one bridge over the river Irwell was nominated by the council for tipping sewage by the night soil men.

These cesspits were stone-lined but were deliberately not waterproof, the idea being that the liquids would filter into the surrounding soil, leaving the relatively solid matter in the pit that was eventually collected by the night soil men. These well-paid souls were also known as rakers, as part of their job was to keep the ditches and streams free of waste using rakes. Often cesspits would be within a few feet of wells or streams used as a source of water. Hardly surprisingly, the water supplies became more and more polluted and plain water was rarely drunk. Instead beer was preferred or, more often, 'small beer', which was boiled water flavoured with dandelions or nettles and left to ferment. Though of a very low alcohol level it was at least fit to drink.

The rich, however, were not too impressed with the situation and from the 1600s there had been schemes to get better quality water into the larger cities, where it could be sold. In 1589 Sir Francis Drake built an 18½-mile leat from a weir on the river Meavy near present day Yelverton down into Plymouth. Originally proposed to water ships, protect against fire, scour the harbour and remove waste from tin works, it soon became Plymouth's main water supply, a task it performed for more than 300 years until 1898.

Though he didn't start the scheme, Hugh Myddelton will be remembered for constructing the 'new river', finished in 1613, from springs in Hertfordshire, 42 miles into north London. The water ran down a meandering canal some 10 ft wide and 4 ft deep, which clung to the contours and eventually reached the Round Pond in Islington, having fallen just 17½ ft from its source. From here it was distributed via elm pipes beneath the streets, with copper pipes feeding into the houses of those who subscribed to the service. It had been an enormous undertaking for its

Wooden water pipes, hewn out of a tree trunk with, a nailed-on lid. (Abbey Pumping Station Museum)

time and indeed when nearly finished Myddelton ran out of money and was rescued by none other than the king himself who took shares in the undertaking and financed its completion.

These long, gravity-fed leats could not simply be turned on and off as needed, so instead a large pond was constructed into which the water ran

Joints were very crude, a taper was formed at one end and pushed into the next section. (Abbey Pumping Station Museum)

and from which the various supplies were taken. The pond acted as a reservoir supplying the peak demand and recovering in the quiet times such as at night. If the pond was found to be overflowing excessively, then the feed from the springs would be adjusted. The demand grew steadily, and in 1713 a steam engine was erected to pump water from the river Lea to supplement the springs.

Incidentally, two-thirds of this water was originally to be used for flushing down the streets and ditches into the ever-polluted river Thames. Today, though much altered and straightened – it is now barely 21 miles long with much of it under cover – its water still flows into the London ring main. Many cities built similar schemes taking clean river water and feeding it via a carefully graded leat into the

The original course of the New River through Enfield. This section was bypassed through a pipe in the 1920s but this was damaged in the war and the original route was brought back into use until 1950. It is now an attractive static feature of the town park.

town, where it was distributed via wooden or earthenware pipes. Often these works would be financed by the town councils who erected taps in the streets at which people could fill their containers before carrying them home. One problem with the early wooden pipes was leakage which was so bad that the water supplies were usually turned on for just a few hours two or three times a week. Each house had its own means of storing water. By the early 1800s iron pipework was used to replace the old elm pipes and slowly through the 1800s water supplies were kept on for longer, until by 1900 it was normal for the water to be on all the time.

There was irony in the improvements made in agriculture during this period; the better stock, seeds and methods, and the ever-improving machinery during the late 1700s, meant more food was produced by the same number of workers. As the rural population grew, there simply was no employment for the extra people, so they had to choose between poverty or seeking paid work in the cities. This steady influx, plus the natural increase in the existing population, meant the cities grew ever faster. Housing for these often desperate workers was thrown up in incredible quantities but most was of pretty poor quality. Many modest houses were hastily converted to permit each room to be let to an entire family; the inevitable squalor can easily be imagined. Often a single privy along with a solitary water tap served a whole row of houses.

Superb Victorian grandeur – the restored James Watt beam engines which drive pumps at Papplewick. These raised water from a bore hole sunk into Bunter sandstone near Nottingham. (Papplewick Pumping Station)

Clean water fed from some far-off spring or stream was still a luxury. Most city water was provided by pumping from wells or a local stream, using a donkey gin which drove simple pumps to lift the water to storage on higher ground from where it could be fed by gravity to the streets. The steam engine now also starts to slowly appear in the water supply industry, pumping much larger quantities of water from the rivers and wells to high-level reservoirs. This approach was needed as the pumps were very basic; their pressure depended on the flow. Had the pumps fed the early wooden pipework directly, then when the demand was low the pumps would be producing too much pressure and the pipes would burst. By feeding the pipes from a reservoir the pressure is constant and if no water is needed the surplus can be safely run off from the reservoir until the pumps are slowed down. Many stately homes installed pumps to feed their own water supplies, though the sewage problem remained, relieved for the wealthy by servants doing the disposing! One oddity – the water closet – was developed in 1778 by Joseph Bramah, but it was way ahead of its time. Very few houses had a suitable water supply and even fewer had a suitable means of getting rid of the waste. Incidentally, the name of this now universal device has always posed a problem. The term 'toilet', from the French *toilette*, means the general process of washing, grooming and dressing. 'Lavatory' simply means to wash, whereas the word 'closet' tends to conjure a room rather than the actual lavatory. Perhaps the Victorians were too prudish to contemplate

devising a specific word and since then we have simply misused other words.

Disease at this time was still rife. Smallpox was the most feared, though thankfully Jenner's discovery of vaccination using cow pox, despite being initially ridiculed, became accepted after 1800. Fevers like typhoid also raged sporadically, invariably borne by poor water and sanitation, though nobody at the time understood this connection.

During the whole period covered in this book there was another change quietly taking place that can make

Typical two-up, two-down terraced cottage of the late 18th century, the rent for which could be afforded by a well-paid worker, foreman or supervisor. Both the front and rear doors would open directly into the rooms and there would be just a small rear yard but no garden.

A poor area in Market Harborough with a typical communal privy in an outbuilding serving 36 residents. Though, strictly, this photograph is outside the period, it conveys a feeling of the cramped conditions. (Abbey Pumping Station Museum)

1850 he would be comfortably established in a small terrace house or cottage and by 1900 he would expect a reasonable two-bedroom house or a good size cottage. The workshop would still be nearby or next door but now work was work and home was home. This change affected all strata of society – even the very poorest who would have progressed from dreadful hovels to Victorian slums and then eventually to relatively comfortable council housing. Incidentally, most people rented their accommodation (over 90 per cent in the mid 1800s) and it wasn't until the 20th century that home ownership spread. Though investment in the many new industries was rewarding, the building of houses, however poor in quality, was seen as a safer option and still produced a return of 7 to 10 per cent.

Early heating depended on wood, whether scraps collected in the local lanes or massive logs from the estate woodlands for the well-to-do. Coal was established for heating in areas like Newcastle, where the poor collected loose coal on the beaches, but it produced a sulphurous smoke and until combustion was better understood it produced little heat. Coal was shipped to large cities like London but being heavy and dirty it was expensive to move far from the docks. The change came in the last decades of the 18th century with the ability of the canals to supply coal to rural towns at a low price. Local coal merchants sprang up and served their own areas, delivering by horse drawn carts. Storage and the inevitable dirt were problems but, with wood becoming more and more difficult to come by in the towns and cities, coal was taking over.

our view of the past confusing. We have as a society become more wealthy and our aspirations have steadily increased. If we take, for instance, a blacksmith – a skilled and essential job right up to the 1930s – and look at the type of house he would live in, we see an improvement that reflects the entire population. In 1750 he would most likely have lived at his place of work, what today we would probably think of as a posh shed! By 1800 he may well have aspired to a small brick-built house, still attached to the workshop. By

CHAPTER 2

The Crackle of the Fire

L ighting in the home was the province of the candle as it had been since Roman times. The simplest and cheapest form used in the home was the rush light, made from rushes cut down in late summer when at their full height but still green. The outer skin was pealed off, itself not an easy task, leaving a rather frail inner skin supporting a soft pith. These were then dried in the sun and stored. When needed the rush was placed in pan of hot tallow to which could be added a small quantity of beeswax. The fat-soaked rushes were then laid out to dry, often on pieces of bark. Tallow was produced from animal fat rendered down and strained to remove material that would otherwise go putrid. Beef tallow was

Rush light holder. (Blaise Castle Museum)

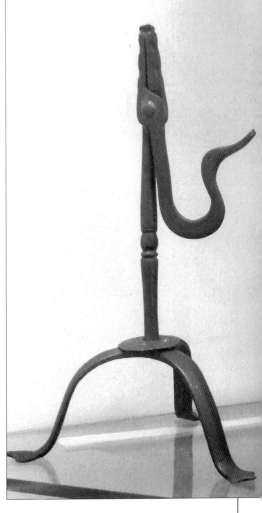

A label from a pack of candles featuring ridges at the base to provide a better grip in the candle holder. (Blaise Castle Museum)

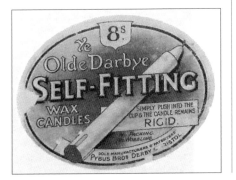

A pair of candle holders in fine china, which may have only rarely seen service. (Think Tank)

the most common but, if one could afford it, sheep tallow was used, as it produced a harder, less sticky candle wax. Pig fat was rarely used as it produced a wax that burns with a lot of smoke and a foul smell. The frail

rush light was held in a simple clip with just a few inches projecting. This would burn with a pale light for maybe 10 to 15 minutes. The clamp was then released and more of the rush moved up to continue burning.

Candles had been made for centuries, and, though beeswax made by far the best, it was expensive and was used mainly by the church. At home tallow candles were the normal source of light and, though some people made their own, the majority bought their candles from the candle maker. Indeed, after 1709 it was illegal to make candles at home and candle makers were taxed until 1831. The candle maker often also produced

The candle maker's workshop. Each beam holds a quantity of wicks, which are dipped into the molten wax, then lifted out to dry on the rotating frame. This is repeated until the wax has built up to the thickness required. (Ironbridge – Blists Hill Victorian Town)

In a different league are these beautiful silver candlesticks. Much favoured in murder mysteries, they would have been used only for very special occasions. (Think Tank)

This is an ingenious adjustable holder that allows the candle to be raised as it burns down. The tab (in the second gap from the base) can be pushed up the spiral and this drives the candle higher. The device has the advantage of keeping the candle well supported but if the wax runs down it all becomes very messy. (The Shambles)

Above is an example of a locally-made candle holder whilst right we see a later factory-produced version. (The Shambles)

soap, which again had been around for many centuries and had been made in England since around 1500. London alone had 63 soap factories by 1700 and production continued to grow until it peaked in 1815.

Tallow melts at a relatively low temperature and unless the candle has a thick wick to absorb the melting wax it will soon run down the side of the candle. The thick wick, however, doesn't completely burn away and slowly the remnants of the wick will collect and prevent the candle burning properly. For this reason it was necessary to trim the wick regularly with a pair of special scissors called snuffers. To extinguish the candle a pair of douters was used, rather like a pair of scissors but with flat metal plates which imitated the action of the fingers in snubbing out a flame.

Though not to be seen in public until after 1800, experiments were already under way to understand coal gas, which was to slowly take over as the main means of providing light. It was discovered almost by accident as one of the by-products of baking coal in an oven to make tar. Several people had worked on this process, both here and in Paris, but it took two very different people to launch the industry. William Murdoch is usually held to be the first person to carry out scientific experiments to understand the process, including discovering which type of coal and which process produced the best gas. Murdoch had joined the

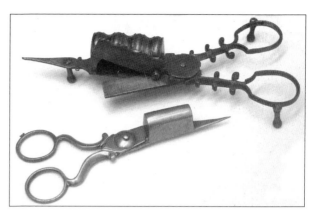

Candle snuffers. Note the small container on the snuffer used to catch the excess wick. (Blaise Castle Museum)

Boulton and Watt Company, primarily supervising the erection of their pumping engines in Cornwall but he possessed a rare mind for solving engineering problems and was always searching for a challenge. He had taken out patents on using tar to preserve the underwater surface of wooden ships and he experimented with distilling tar into various other useful products, work that was eventually to lead to the start of the chemical industry. We shall meet the second person later. There was little interest in Murdoch's work with gas but in 1801 he returned to the task, spurred on by the news of similar work being carried out in France by Philippe Lebon. In 1802 Murdoch, who was able to use the skills and facilities of the Boulton and Watt factory, used gas to illuminate part of the Soho foundry in Birmingham. Over the next three years he tested out many ideas and slowly devised the best way to 'cook' the coal and clean the resultant gas.

CHAPTER 3

The Cities Explode

The population movement from the country to the cities, plus the enormous increase in the natural population in the towns, brought quite unprecedented problems to both the logistics of food supply and the embryo water and waste industries. By the 1820s the factory movement was really getting into its stride, led by the cotton and wool industries. Wedgwood had moved the making of china and earthenware into a production-line process and entrepreneurs like Boulton had led the way in metalwork. Iron was now being produced in enormous quantities and could be supplied as a raw material to small iron works in towns and cities where the local craftsmen would rework it to meet the needs of the local area. The roads were now also showing signs of real improvement. In 1802 Trevithick demonstrated his first steam-driven road vehicle, though it was too heavy for the roads of the time. Tentatively, gas lighting was being provided in a few upper-class streets and the concept of making gas to be distributed around a city was being developed. All this industry was starting to have an unforeseen effect on society. Above the manual workers there was now a much larger layer of doctors, legal men, supervisors, designers and more skilled people who had spare money – some had lots of spare money – thus was born the middle class. This included the more skilled factory workers who could now afford a better diet and could enjoy their Sunday rest from toil, and skilled tradesmen and administrators who found themselves able to live a very comfortable life. A few, lucky or cheeky enough, found themselves making serious money and they would soon aspire to rub shoulders with the landed gentry, who looked down with horror at these wealthy tradespeople. An idea of the speed of this expansion can be gauged from a few figures. London, still the largest city in Europe, went from around 1 million people in 1800 to 2 million by 1840. There were no other cities of over 100,000 souls in 1800 but by 1850 there were nine when Leeds topped 170,000, Birmingham over 230,000 and Manchester an astonishing 300,000.

Vast quantities of sewage were now reaching the rivers via ditches, local streams and leaking cesspits, and though most people believed this pollution had no link to disease it was plainly unpleasant to take water from a well which not only looked dirty but probably smelt as well. The quaintly named 'Inspectors of Nuisances' were appointed to sort out problems like leaking cesspits and waste from slaughterhouses. All this drove the idea of improving water supplies and, over the next 30 years many water companies were formed, who either took their water from deep wells or from the rivers upstream of the cities. Some used sand filtering

A reservoir of 1,500 gallons' capacity erected in 1829 on the initiative of the Youlgreave Friendly Society of Women to provide the village with its first piped water from a spring at Mawstone. This developed into a one-village water company, the smallest water company in the land.

The state of housing, however, was appalling. The speed at which the larger towns were expanding and the need to house thousands of poorly paid workers as cheaply as possible generated slums that almost defy description. Often a family of six or seven would occupy a single room with no fire to heat water or to use for cooking – conditions ripe for disease. In 1842 a survey in Liverpool found 39,000 people living in 7,800 cellars, just a simple cellar for five souls.

Born of the early schemes like the New River, small water companies were forming who would undertake to supply water via a network of pipes to an area of a city. By 1845 London had nine such companies, though by 1850 many had been taken over by the local authorities. A typical early provincial example was the Trent Water Works company who in 1830 under their first engineer, Thomas Hawksley, built basic sand and gravel filter beds beside the river Trent, from where a 40 hp beam engine drove pumps which lifted the filtered river water to a reservoir a mile away.

From this higher ground the water was fed to Nottingham by gravity and though still not really pure enough for drinking it was much cleaner than the river. Though not realized until much later, bacteria developed in the sand, which fed on the harmful organic material in the water, making it purer than the simple mechanical filtering might have suggested. All these improvements were aided by the new cast-iron pipes which, compared to wooden pipes, were strong, were made in longer sections and were easier to join.

beds and covered the reservoirs to prevent rubbish entering the water. This also prevented the dumping of sewage, which was probably the main reason for covering up clean water! Though supplying individual houses with water was still a long way off, providing plenty of communal pumps and taps was regarded as a service that should be provided free of charge. This was one of the early signs of the influence of the factory owners, who had a vested interest in keeping the workers reasonably fit.

Two communal pumps, the left-hand one might be found beside a road in a small village whereas the right-hand one is a far more serious piece of machinery requiring considerable strength to operate. (Black Country Living Museum)

Rubbish was now collected, at least from the well-off areas, and carted away to dust yards, where men, women and children sorted and sifted it, selling on materials they could recycle – all very green! Sewage, though, remained as it ever was.

We must also remember that the problems of water supply and sewage were large town and city phenomena. Out in the country the smaller towns carried on as before, not perfect but not so crowded and cramped. Even here there was change of a sort. The canals, the railways (after the 1830s) and the better roads were doing away with the old problem of transport being difficult and expensive. It didn't matter so much if you had to travel to fetch something or, just as important, if you had something to sell. Farms started to move further from the towns to be in the centre of their lands, with large farms providing meagre housing for the workers that formed a sort of embryo village. For

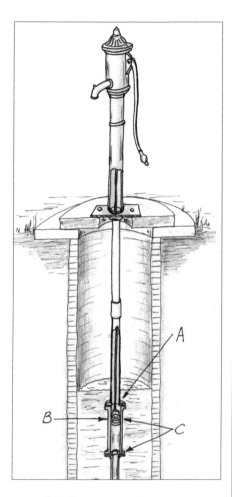

Typical shallow town well.
A. Shaft bolted onto the pump.
B. Piston operated by the rod from the pump handle. C. Valves that prevent the water running out as the pump is operated.

cities. Every week stalls would be set up with the sort of items that weren't made in a small town or large village, items not essential for life but which made it more pleasant, such as cutlery, glassware and china, jewellery, toys and trinkets, fancy clothing like handkerchiefs, scarves, small silk items, and ornaments. Food also featured – produce that wasn't grown locally and with a wider choice of fruit and vegetables. The world was truly shrinking.

Back in the kitchen, the problem of keeping food fresh and away from vermin was solved with the 'safe' – a storage cupboard, with large openings covered in perforated zinc sheeting or sometimes a wire gauze, which allowed air to circulate. These were still in regular use into the 1950s. For the better off, there were ice-boxes, lead-lined cabinets which held ice in the top section and the food below. Ice, imported from North America and Norway, was sold and delivered in most large towns or cities. Home-made bread would be hung from a wooden frame suspended from the ceiling, again to keep it out of reach of vermin.

Coal was by now making an impact on domestic heating. Delivered by horse and cart, it was burned in iron grates of various shapes, many of which were not well designed, thus producing smoke and not much heat. Slowly the designs improved, including the enclosed fireplace as used in the slow burning range, which could use coal as well as the traditional wood. These produced heat not just for warmth but for cooking and heating water. The living room now became the centre of life, where the cooking was done along with the

centuries there had been a system of markets and peddlers, which now grew to form a link between smaller towns and the larger manufacturing

An early photo of poor living conditions in Hereford. The washing would usually be done outside in the communal yard. Note the boarded up windows and those with no glass, both common in slum housing. (The Waterworks Museum)

small wood or coal fire with a simple outside chimney. This heated the water primarily for washing and laundry. In rural areas, if a well with a hand pump supplied the water, then the pump would be near the copper and sink to minimize the need to move water around.

Along with the improvements in the water supply there had been a steady building of sewers but at first these were only for collecting surface water and it was illegal to allow house waste to enter them, a rule regularly broken. In the large cities these were often simply small streams and rivers which were directed into brick-lined tunnels, into which road drains emptied. Possibly because the sewers were being covered over and were more able to handle greater volumes, the 'no sewage' law was repealed in 1815 and households were slowly connected to the sewers. Henry Doulton started his factory in Lambeth in 1846 to manufacture glazed stoneware pipes, primarily for use in building these smaller local sewers. Like all improvements this benefited the better off who could install a water closet, which, unlike ours today, used four or more gallons of water to flush. All this extra water started to produce cleaner sewers but even dirtier rivers.

weekly ritual of bathing. At the back of the house, or often under a lean-to, would be the cold water tap, the washing tub and wringer used for the clothes and, of course, the privy.

The rich would still have their servants to bring hot water from the kitchens in jugs and the toilets would by now be indoors and might feature one of the newfangled water closets. The bathroom, as we think of it, was still a long way off and personal washing was done in a large bowl or basin in the bedroom. Hot water was brought up from the kitchen in a jug or metal can and the waste was poured into another large pot which was taken downstairs to be emptied. In many homes there would be a separate copper in the scullery, consisting of a metal tub built into a brick enclosure. At the bottom was a

The attitude of the Government

throughout this period is interesting. It had little concern for the welfare of the general population. Occasionally it had to admit to their existence when it needed to raise money for some ill-advised war, but it was not until the heads of industry grew in influence that Parliament took any real interest.

When a threat of disease was perceived the Government quickly formed a Board of Health but if the threat passed the Board would be disbanded. Early in our period there was a scare of yellow fever which evoked this response. Soon after there was a serious outbreak of cholera on the Continent and again the Board of Health was formed, only to be disbanded when the disease failed to cross the Channel. It was also popularly believed that diseases spread through the air – it was the stench of foul waste (miasma) that gave you the illness. This belief was widely held and was supported by many eminent people. Right up to her death in 1910, Florence Nightingale was adamant that this was how

An early wood-burning grate, with various pots and pans with the gadgets to hold them over the fire. (Cogges Manor Farm Museum)

disease spread. Unfortunately, as we will see, it took three cholera outbreaks and a terrified Parliament before anything serious was done to combat the cause of the disease.

Cholera spread, it is believed, from India, reaching our shores in 1831. It spread quickly, within the first nine

Victorian wash stand, with jugs and waste water carrier.

months 22,000 people had died, and it was soon found in most parts of the land. A cruel disease that killed sometimes in less than a day, it provoked all the usual theories that followed a disease that was not understood.

In 1842 the Poor Law Commission issued a report into the sanitary conditions of the poor, based largely on the findings of its secretary, Edwin Chadwick. The report was just as horrifying as earlier revelations but this time it came with the authority

Opposite. An open-fronted cast-iron range as would be found in many 1840s cottages. Fuelled by wood or coal, it heated both the oven at the side and water. Always the centre of activity, it quickly became surrounded by all manner of handy odds and ends. (Black Country Living Museum)

Scullery with water pump and copper in the corner, complete with small fire hole at the bottom. Nearest the camera is a wooden mangle. Many children could tell the story of getting their fingers caught in the rollers as they fed in the clothes. (The Shambles)

and drive of Chadwick, a very aggressive and industrious man who had trained as a barrister. One of its findings was that the life expectancy for the upper classes was an average of 43 years, for tradesmen 30 years and for labourers a lowly 22 years, and this was barely 165 years ago! The result was the creation of the first permanent General Board of Health, set up under the Public Health Act of 1848. At last, someone was taking the supply of water and the disposal of sewage seriously. Just a year later another massive outbreak of cholera took over 50,000 lives, 14,000 of them in London alone.

Dr John Snow, an anaesthetist, a profession then in its infancy, had become interested in cholera during the previous outbreaks and studied the spread of the disease. He soon became convinced that water was the carrier. In the 1854 outbreak he had realized that most of the affected houses in the part of Soho where he worked took their water from one particular pump. After some pleading he was able to get the pump handle removed to prevent any further use and the outbreak in the area promptly died down. Later inspection showed the well was close to a poorly-built sewer. Though he had written up his findings, little was done, but his work was to have immense importance.

CHAPTER 4

Let There Be Light – Gas Arrives

William Murdoch's success in lighting the Soho foundry using gas was not lost on industrialists who were anxious to rid themselves of oil and candles in their factories. Not only was there the obvious risk of fire but due to Napoleon's blockade of goods from Russia and Scandinavia, which included vast quantities of tallow, the price of candles had virtually doubled at the start of the 19th century. Approached by Lee and Philips, who had just constructed one of the two largest mills in England, Boulton and Watt supplied a complete gas system to light the mill. Starting with 50 lights in January 1806 and soon expanding to 904, these proved brighter than candles or oil lamps and were more economical (the 904 gas lights had replaced 2,500 oil lamps). Very soon Murdoch and Boulton were producing gas-making plants for use in other mills. They were not alone in this work but they certainly led the way. In Paris, Philippe Lebon had pioneered work primarily aimed at lighting streets and homes but, alas, he was murdered in the Champs-Elysées in 1804.

Enter our second pioneer of gas, the strange character of Friedrich Winzer from Moravia, who was a mix of over-enthusiastic entrepreneur and con man. He had followed Lebon's work in Paris, becoming quite a nuisance to Lebon who had seen lighting the streets of Paris as his main market. Winzer then came to England in 1803 to try and further his ideas. He changed his name to Winsor and commenced a massive publicity campaign, even taking over the Lyceum theatre to demonstrate a wonderful array of gas lights. Though undoubtedly a marketing man rather than an engineer, he had grasped one fundamental idea from the start – the profit from gas lay not in its production but in its distribution and selling. He always saw gas as something to be made in a factory and then piped around a city and fed to individual shops and houses in the same way as water. After a few more bold publicity stunts he attempted to form the New Patriotic Imperial and National Light and Heat Company, a title that perhaps gives us a clue to Winsor's character. He was soon able to attract a group of shrewd backers and then attempted to get a virtual monopoly of gas supply but was defeated by, among others, Boulton and Watt.

By now the Boulton and Watt Company was run by the sons of the original founders, who unfortunately lacked the spirit of adventure of their

Memory of a once-common street name. (Fakenham Museum of Gas)

fathers. Though fully aware of the rival company's ideas to distribute gas, they still failed to grasp the opportunity despite having great knowledge of producing gas and also real experience in distributing it over fairly large areas in the mills. They finally withdrew from the gas business completely in 1815.

So, Winsor and his backers managed to obtain a virtual monopoly of gas lighting in London for 21 years and, in 1812, formed the Gas Light and Coke Company, which was to remain one of the leading gas companies right up to 1949, when the industry was nationalized. Winsor continued to make wild claims and became something of an embarrassment to the company he helped form and he was duly sacked. He returned to France, partly to flee creditors, and attempted to start a new company but that failed and sadly he died in relative obscurity in 1830.

Throughout the period covered by this book gas meant 'town gas' and as the name suggests town gas was made locally in the individual towns. In the larger cities there would be many gas works owned by several different companies. In fact, at nationalization

there were still over 1,000 independent gas companies. Because the manufacture of town gas ceased over 50 years ago and the works that made it have all disappeared (bar one small preserved site in Norfolk), I thought I should divert here to look at the processes involved. This didn't directly affect the domestic life at home but before the advent of North Sea gas everyone knew where their gas works was, and indeed many older people will still remember being taken to their local works when they had whooping cough, as the fumes were believed to help loosen the cough.

The process of making gas is basically very simple: coal is heated in a sealed retort where it is baked at over 1,000°C. The seal is achieved by a tight fitting cast-iron door, as it is vital to prevent oxygen reaching the coal which must not be allowed to catch fire and burn. The cooking releases a hot, thick, smelly gas containing tar, ammonia and other minor gases, plus the gas required for lighting and heating. At the end of this cooking, the coal is reduced to coke which is almost pure carbon. Early retorts were made of cast-iron but these suffered from the heat and

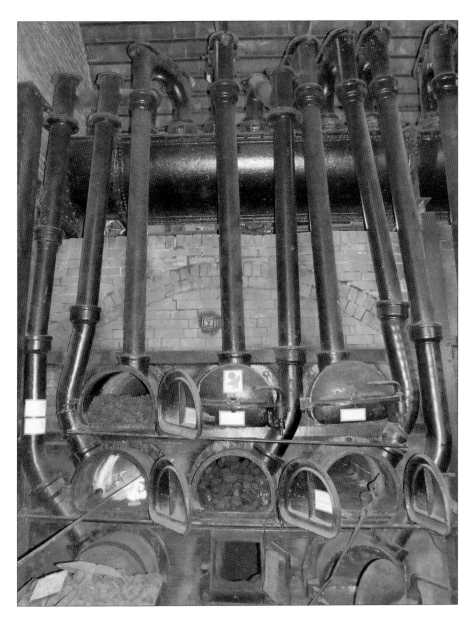

One of the two banks of retorts in a typical small town gas works. The furnace is fed via the single square door (bottom centre). The middle row shows a retort being emptied, a retort full of new coal and an empty retort. (Fakenham Museum of Gas)

The washer removed the ammonia. (Fakenham Museum of Gas)

quite early in the 1800s long, flat tunnel retorts built of fire bricks and clay were introduced. Several of these were built around a fire whose flames and hot gases rose around the retorts. The whole structure took a long time to reach the necessary high temperature and so it was normal practice to keep the furnace going and just open the retorts to extract the coke at the end of a 'cook' and refill them with fresh coal. A 'cook' took around 8 hours, so most works ran on a 24-hour basis with two 12-hour shifts, the men being able to rest between their two or three hour sessions.

As one can imagine, emptying and loading the retorts was extremely hot and dirty work, though later larger works used mechanical rakes to empty the coke. The coke, of course, was still red hot at this stage and was watered down immediately, partly to make the working area cooler but also to stop the coke igniting now that it had access to oxygen. During the 'cook' the gases which erupted from the coal rose up large pipes to the top of the furnace structure where there was a long tank holding water. Each pipe turned over and dipped into the water through which the gases bubbled. The water acted as a seal to prevent gas passing back down to a retort which was being reloaded, whilst the water cooled the gases, causing the tar to condense out. The tar ran along the bottom of the sloping tank and was collected and piped to a holding tank. Outside the retort house the gas would be passed through a further condenser, cooling it further and removing the remaining tar.

Next came the exhauster which drew the gas from the retorts and pumped it on its way, followed by the washer where the gas was bubbled up through water to dissolve out the ammonia. Later on, this stage was followed by a scrubber where the gas passed through trays of wet coke. Lastly, the hydrogen sulphide was removed by passing the gas through trays of iron oxide, after which the quantity of gas produced was measured by the station meter before it went into the gas holder.

The use of the word gasometer for these devices is incorrect but has been there from the start and may have taken hold for a rather strange reason. In the first twenty or so years

The condenser from the restored Fakenham works, which would remove the last of the tar. (Fakenham Museum of Gas)

of gas making, there was no reliable way to measure the amount of gas being made or sold, so filling a gas holder of known size provided a measure of how much gas had been made. If there where two holders,

The last stage, where the hydrogen sulphide was removed by passing it over trays holding iron oxides. The valves in the centre of the picture allowed for a section to be isolated to allow the trays to be removed and cleaned before being replaced. (Fakenham Museum of Gas)

then whilst one was filling the other could be used to supply the gas mains, giving a measure of how much gas had been supplied. Gas meters (gas-ometers) were eventually made but the term stuck in the popular mind as the name of the holders.

Still used only for lighting public buildings and streets, plus the occasional private house, the gas was burnt from a ceramic burner as a lazy yellow flame. Initially the lamp lighter carried a ladder, up which he climbed at each street lamp to light the flame. Fairly quickly the idea of a small pilot flame was introduced and all the lamp lighter had to do was turn on the gas tap to the main light, a task that only needed a long pole from the ground.

In the 1840s it was realized that by mixing air with the gas it burned much more efficiently, a principle used in every gas fire or cooker ever since. This process was developed by Michael Faraday, not Bunsen as is so often quoted.

By 1850 many cities and large towns had a gas works, usually near a railway or canal, where the coal could be supplied economically. Still seen in a few larger towns, the gas holders were the most dominant feature of the gas works. Because of the process it was not possible to increase the output from the retorts to cope with peaks in demand but it made sense to keep the works going 24 hours a day, thus still making gas in the night. The gas holders were designed to act as reservoirs, storing the gas and absorbing the ups and downs in demand. They were basically large upturned tin cans which sat in a deep pool of water. The water provided the

Two of the seven remaining gas holders in Birmingham. This lighter lattice-style construction was very common in later years.

Gas holders. Still in use in Macclesfield, this fairly early single lift holder has cast-iron pillars to form the support structure.

Two massive spiral holders beside the river Thames in Reading. Each spiral is held in guides and thus provides the section with much more support than simple vertical runners. This meant that it was possible to dispense with the outside support frames.

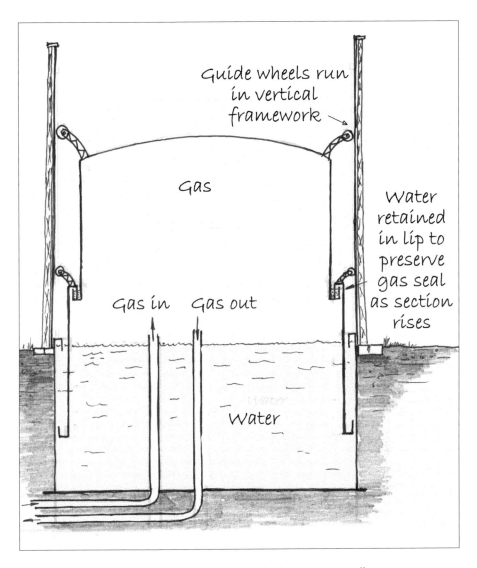

Diagram to show how the 'upside-down tins' actually sit in deep water. This two-lift holder is shown three-quarters full, with the top section, in effect, pulling the lower section up.

seal preventing the gas from escaping and the 'tin can' was able to rise and fall as the gas came and went, held by a giant framework which kept the gas holder vertical.

From the start it was iron pipework which made the piping of gas around a town practical and before long there were miles and miles of gas mains under the streets of every city. In houses the use of gas was limited to lighting and even though it was now mixed with air the flame still provided plenty of soot on the ceiling and a slight smell. It took until the mid 1800s to develop a reliable gas meter, so in the beginning households were charged by the number of lights in their house and inspectors could visit to make sure they hadn't added any more!

An early gas meter designed to measure gas in cubic feet. (Milestones)

The Westminster gas works has an interesting history. Opened in 1813, it soon expanded and by 1840 it had four retort houses and some 20 small gas holders. By 1850 the site had been extended again and two large conventional gas holders were erected. After the works closed in 1875 (the site by then was too small and the land was valuable), the two gas holders were kept just for storage until 1937, when the entire site was

cleared apart from the gas holders which were to see a rather novel use. The two massive water pits, some 50 ft deep, were used as the basis for the underground bombproof offices used by the War Cabinet. On top of this they built the three towers of the Department of the Environment. When this was eventually demolished in 2002 the circular shapes of the offices were briefly revealed.

CHAPTER 5

Coal to Heat the Nation

Following the arrival of the railways, the use of coal for heating houses grew apace. The iron industries duly responded with a wonderful range of grates and ranges.

This roof-top scene from central London shows no fewer than 29 chimney pots of several designs, reflecting repairs over the years.

Early sinks were either lead-lined wood or, as here, stoneware. This one has patterned edges. There would be no drain in many houses at this time and the water would be emptied into a large bucket and taken to the vegetable patch if possible. (Ironbridge – Blists Hill Victorian Town)

The way a chimney worked became better understood, some early ideas including the well-known inglenook produced smoke in all directions. The realization that it was the temperature of the smoke that caused it to rise led to the idea of keeping the smoke hot whilst in the chimney. Older chimneys had been built large enough to permit young boys to climb up inside to clean them (banned in 1828) but this produced a vast volume and unless a really large fire was burning the smoke simply cooled down before reaching the top and effectively blocked the chimney.

Starting a new fire in these large chimney grates was an awful problem for the same reason. Overcoming this was achieved by making its journey fast by using a small-sized chimney, thus reducing the time during which the smoke could lose its heat. So successful was this technique that the air drawn through the fire by the upward surge would have the fire burning furiously within minutes unless deliberately controlled. Various designs of dampers (sometimes referred to as registers) were built into the fireplace or chimneys which allowed the fire to be controlled.

The coal fire became a relatively safe method of heating and cooking which was commonplace right up to the 1960s. Middle-class houses were built with a cast-iron fireplace in the living room and sometimes in the bedrooms. Each fire had its own chimney, resulting in the multiple chimney pots we can still see today on older houses. Originally there were no chimney pots but the turbulence caused by the chimney structure hindered the smoke from being carried away and on still days smoke from one fire could roll across the top and drift back down into another unlit fireplace.

All these chimneys needed sweeping, as the soot from burning coal would stick to the insides of the chimney stack just as it had in the older, wide chimneys. It was usual to have the chimneys swept every year, involving

quite a performance. The sweep would lay a sheet around the fireplace and then feed the brush up the chimney, screwing on another 6 ft section as needed until the brush popped out of the chimney pot. He would then bring the brush back down, unscrewing the extensions as he went, until all the loose soot had fallen into the grate. If the roof allowed, sometimes the sweep would reverse the process. Standing on the roof he would lower the brush down the chimney, pulled down by an iron weight. Soot was a useful commodity in gardening, as digging some into the soil got rid of slugs and snails and other plant-eating pests. In rural areas it was common to use a small tree, rather like a Christmas tree, instead of a brush.

By the end of our period (1850) most larger towns and cities had piped water, at least in the more well-off areas, and sewers as we think of them were being built. The advent of piped water meant the arrival of the sink with its solitary cold water tap. The really well-off would now have a flushing toilet and its waste, plus that from the sink, would now go into the sewers. Gas lighting would also feature in these well-off areas and we can start to imagine the birth of the relatively comfortable early Victorian house. The vast majority of people, though, were simply rejoicing in having possibly two taps and even two privies per terrace of houses instead of just one, plus a few gas lights on the main streets. Candles still provided the domestic lighting and, as in rural areas, the idea of the utility industries was still a dream. Only a single fire provided heat for cooking and heating water, and the

Restored kitchen from the early 1800s, which is still used on special demonstration days. This is typical of the well-off country gentleman's home.
(Cogges Manor Farm Museum)

chances were that most of the windows and doors let draughts in with gay abandon.

The hundred years between 1750 and 1850 had produced an amazing range of new ideas and discoveries. Some, like the mechanization of farming and the canals, had grown to be mature and successful industries. Some, like clean water, sewage disposal and gas lighting, still lacked a clear purpose to justify their costs. The list of domestic inventions that still awaited that magical step between bright idea and profitable product was long and varied. The pressure cooker had been demonstrated to royalty in 1680, the mercury thermometer arrived in 1715, the first successful false teeth in 1770 and by 1810 tinned food was available. The first sewing machines were in production in 1830, the first safety match in 1845 and the refrigerator was designed in 1834. Rumbling quietly in the background during this period were experiments with electricity, climaxing in the development by John Daniel in 1836 of a successful wet battery cell.

SECTION
II

1850 – 1900

CHAPTER 6

Cholera Strikes Again

T he optimistic air at the end of chapter 5 was, alas, short-lived, the General Board of Health being wound up in 1858. An article in *The Times* showed how Chadwick's aggressive attitude had upset the population, commenting that 'it would prefer to take its chance of cholera and the rest than to be bullied into health'. Various Health Acts had been passed and, though there was still no proven links between poor drinking water and disease, the water companies were obliged to keep water covered and free from contamination. In the meantime, the rivers in the large cities were becoming literally open sewers. Travelling by river was now a means of last resort so bad was the stench. We must also remember that the miasmic theory of disease being spread via the stench from rotting waste was still firmly in favour and it was this that provided the push in London to do something about the sewers. Only subsequently did the existence of water-borne disease and the dangers of sewage become apparent.

The year 1858 turned out to have a very hot summer, so hot that the Members of Parliament retreated from the main chambers to get away from the dreadful smell of the Thames. Thus, unable to pretend any more that all was well, they finally agreed to

The pump house and storage chambers under construction at Crossness. Extensive use was made of concrete in these works. (Thames Water)

underwrite the vast expense of completely modernizing London's sewers. Masterminded by Joseph Bazalgette, a completely new set of sewers was built running parallel to the Thames and intercepting the old sewers on their way to the river. Giant pumps then raised the sewage so that it could continue its journey by gravity down the Thames valley before being pumped into the river near Becton on the north shore and Crossness on the south. To prevent the sewage drifting back into London on the tide, enormous covered holding tanks were built at Becton and Crossness and the stored sewage was only released into the river when the tide was flowing out to sea.

The Joseph Bazalgette memorial on the Thames embankment in London. Like Brunel he was one of those rare people who could grasp the total picture whilst still controlling the detail.

Constructed between 1858 and 1866 this was an amazing feat of engineering and political will. Thousands of slum dwellings were cleared to be replaced by new roads under which the new sewers plied their task. The two Thames embankments were constructed partly to carry the new main sewers but also to provide railway lines and ducts for water, gas and, later, electricity cables. Most of London's bridges were improved or rebuilt; the upheaval must have been astonishing but as a result the Thames started its long journey back to being a normal clean river. There was just one section near the river Lea, however, which was to prove pivotal to our story. By 1866 the pumps at Abbey Mills, near West Ham, were not complete and when a fourth outbreak of cholera struck London the river Lea became the unfortunate recipient of the waste

from areas such as Bow. This was the one area still to be connected to the new sewers. Due to lax management, the East London Water Company had failed to fully comply with the appropriate Water Acts and contamination from the Lea had entered their drinking water system, and despite protesting their innocence they were found to be guilty. There had been some 4,363 deaths, of which 93 per cent were within the area supplied by the East London Company. The fact that so few had been infected where the sewage was being removed via the new sewers and so many had died within the area supplied by just one company stood as even more proof that cholera was water-borne. Quickly the importance of keeping clean water completely separate from the sewerage system became accepted throughout the land. The professional operation of these two utilities was accepted as vital and though the treatment has altered over the centuries Victorian sewers still serve most of the large cities in the UK.

Pictorial cross-section of the Thames embankment near Charing Cross station.

Though the mechanism was still not fully understood, it was noted that outbreaks of typhoid also dropped dramatically. By 1872 the death rate in London, still the world's largest city, was lower than almost anywhere else in the world. In 1883 Robert Koch, an eminent German bacteriologist, identified the cholera bacillus and established that it was indeed carried in water. Despite all this, in 1893, two respected chemists working in public health declared that they believed that neither cholera or typhoid germs could survive in sewage and declared their fervent belief in the miasmic theory – you can't keep a popular theory down!

In 1896 there was a further outbreak of cholera on the Continent, being particularly bad in Hamburg. Though the authorities quietly held their breath, there was no epidemic in the UK. Some 130 probable cases occurred around the country but most of these

Giant steam-driven beam engines were the usual choice for pumping sewage because of their plodding reliability. These magnificent machines have been preserved at the Abbey Pumping Station in Leicester and are occasionally in steam. (Abbey Pumping Station Museum)

DEATH'S DISPENSARY
Open to the Poor, Gratis, by Permission of the Parish

The satirical press often got closer to the truth than the politicians. This famous cartoon from Fun *magazine makes no mistake over water-borne diseases.*

victims were found to have travelled from the Continent shortly before their illness. It is amazing that our two most basic utilities were born not of a desire for clean water or an understanding of disease but as a response to the disgusting condition of the country's rivers. Gas and electricity were much simpler, both were straightforward sources of energy, made as a commercial venture from the start.

Part of Bazalgette's main sewers being inspected. Judging by the sunlight on the right we must be fairly near the surface. (Thames Water)

CHAPTER 7

The Cosy Victorian Home

Our domestic story now enters a period of steady improvements both in health and in comfort. Various Health Acts now required new housing to be built

A scullery, with the washday apparel. Note the built-in copper, and just showing in the bottom corner is the edge of a small coal-fired range.
(Black Country Living Museum)

*The local market.
This scene is of Lower
Parliament Street in
Nottingham, long
since redeveloped.*
(Picture the Past)

*Gas mantles and a
three-jet ceramic
burner.* (Fakenham
Museum of Gas)

with connections to both sewers and drinking water. The spacing between buildings and various construction techniques were all laid down in building regulations. Our typical middle-class house in the cities and larger towns would be very pleasant. The living room would still be the centre of life, with a coal fire, possibly in a range, for cooking and heating water, and for keeping the room warm. There would be a scullery with cool food storage, a sink with a single cold water tap, a scrubbing board for washing clothes and possibly a wringer or mangle. Keeping food cool had

developed into a well-practised technique using cupboards with ventilation on outside walls and, if possible, with floors laid directly onto the ground beneath the house. When Billingsgate meat market was rebuilt in the 1850s the design of the roof and the ventilation alone kept the inside temperature at least 10° cooler than the outside temperature. The absence of domestic refrigeration before the 1950s was the reason for so many local food shops and butchers; one simply shopped nearly every day for things like milk and meat. In these days of logistics and large lorries we forget that in the 1800s meat slaughtered, hung and ready on Monday was in the markets by Tuesday morning and in the butchers' shops by Wednesday. Milk, fruit and vegetables were handled just as swiftly.

Gas lighting would provide a somewhat dim but welcome light in the main rooms and the hallway. In 1875 Carl Auer invented the luminescent gas mantle, in recognition of which he was given the title Carl Auer von Welsbach. He set up his first mantle-making factory in London in

A selection of early soaps, including some of the well-known brand names like Pears. (Abbey Pump Museum)

Shops catered for most needs. Here, a general provisions shop which would one day grow into a supermarket! (The Shambles)

Cold room on a north corner of the house, with stone slab floor. (Cogges Manor Farm Museum)

All very cosy: sash windows, somewhere to dry the clothes, gas lights and hot water and warmth. (Black Country Living Museum)

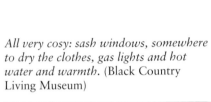

Two examples of water-filter jars, one from Greenhalgh's of Rochdale, the other from the British Pasteur Chamberland Filter Company. (Cogges Manor Farm Museum and Milestones)

1877, producing relatively tough mantles coated in thorium and cerium oxides, which lasted for 2,000 hours or more. The mantle covered the gas flame and, driven by the heat, the fragile coating gave off a bright clear white light ten times as bright as the early open flame gas lights. This one event allowed the gas light to stay a viable competitor to the new electric light right up into the 1950s. The first mantles were fitted over the gas flame, pointing upwards, but by 1900 mantles which could work facing downwards were produced and from this time gas lamps always hung down allowing the best spread of light.

It was during this period that most of the old back-to-back slums were cleared away and, in more respectable areas, the four or five storey Victorian terraces were built. With two rooms per floor they were actually very badly designed, the endless staircase consuming nearly a fifth of the entire volume. These were the houses of the aspiring middle classes, with a maid whose life consisted in the main of climbing and descending stairs! Throughout the 1800s it had become popular for the middle classes to have water filters at home even after more reliable piped water arrived. These were jars, made in a wide range of sizes, containing carbon as the filtering agent – there's nothing new!

In rural areas and away from the large towns life would also be getting more comfortable but the lavatory would still be an outside privy, lighting would still be candles or oil lamps and the water would still be carried in from a well or stream.

The one oddity was the rich man's country house, invariably set in large grounds and well away from any form of water, sewage or gas supplies. Money compensated, however, and often water from a river or stream would be pumped to a small reservoir on higher ground, from which the house was supplied. If you were really rich you might even have a small

self-contained gas works to provide gas lighting. These installations seem to have not only disappeared from the buildings but also from the memory. Many grand National Trust houses proudly display great chandeliers that originally used gas but the only remaining trace of these small gas works is in Culzean Castle in Scotland and even there all the machinery has gone. Coal and wood still provided the heating and servants still made the unpleasant rituals of toilet disposal bearable. Even if the end product was destined to be fed into a large cesspit it could be taken there in pipes which acted as 'local' sewers permitting water closets to be provided. Hot water was still brought from the kitchens in jugs.

Another item now became a regular purchase – soap. Known for a very long time, it works because of its peculiar molecule, one end of which is

Most soap was still supplied cut from bars and sold by weight. (The Shambles)

attracted to water (hydrophilic) whilst the other is repelled by water (hydrophobic). The non-water-loving end attaches to dirt and bacteria whilst the other end strives to get into the water, thus dragging the dirt off the surface being washed. Soap also reduces surface tension in water, which permits the water to enter small crevices more freely and again aids cleaning. Andrew Pears began making transparent soap in 1789 by dissolving soap in alcohol, then distilling the alcohol to leave a transparent jelly which was then set in moulds. Soap was heavily taxed and by 1815 was carrying virtually 100 per cent tax.

At the 1851 Great Exhibition there were no fewer than 727 companies showing soap products. Gladstone finally repealed the tax in 1853, by which time Britain was producing some 60,000 tons of soap a year. Most soap was still sold by weight, being cut from a large bar rather like cheese. Brand names started to appear which we still know today: Pears, Knights, Gibbs and Yardley were all around in the 1850s and Pears in particular engaged in massive advertising campaigns.

The razor, that basic bathroom

The cut-throat razor, often sold in boxes of seven to serve the week. (Milestones)

The classic Victorian shaving stand for the gentleman of the house.

(Top) The slipper bath in which one sat almost completely immersed in water. The term 'slipper' still lingered on in public baths long after this type of tub disappeared. (Below) The more common hip bath, still in use in rural areas in the 20th century. (Abbey Pumping Station Museum and The Shambles)

item, had for centuries been the open cut-throat type and indeed during much of the 18th and 19th centuries men were often shaved by a barber. By 1762 a safety version had been marketed but it wasn't until King C. Gillette developed the modern safety razor in 1903 that shaving became less hazardous.

The bath had made intermittent appearances over the years, normally only associated with the very rich, but slowly through the mid 1800s they started to appear in middle-class homes as well. In 1837 when Queen Victoria

Gas-heated bath from around 1870. The gas burner is at floor level, nearest the camera. It was swung out to be lit (once there was water in the bath) and was then pushed back under the bath. (Blaise Castle Museum)

entered Buckingham Palace there was not a single bath anywhere in the palace. It is interesting to note that many designs of this period incorporated a shower, a feature that was to fall out of fashion in the 1920s. Bathing was still seen primarily as a health giving treatment and the idea of a bath being just a pleasurable way to keep clean didn't develop until well into the 1880s. Adverts for baths always referred to the 'patient' rather than the user. The problem with the bath was not just how to supply enough water but also how to heat it.

This last problem was tackled with a wonderful array of coal and gas-fired devices that warmed the bath itself or were immersed in the bath water until it was warm enough for bathing. Slowly the gas-powered water heater developed, Benjamin Waddy Maughan producing the first so-called geyser in 1868. In the beginning many designs resembled large tea urns but the fumes and soot caused endless problems. In 1880 the first cast-iron baths were produced and the bath became a mass-production item. Still very heavy and cold until the hot water got to

a.

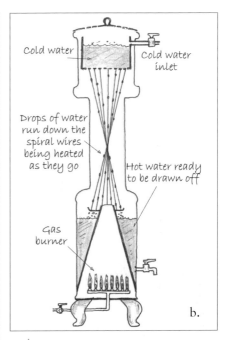

Cold water

Cold water inlet

Drops of water run down the spiral wires being heated as they go

Hot water ready to be drawn off

Gas burner

b.

(a) The first Maughan geyser, from 1868, and (b) a cross-section showing how it worked. There was absolutely nothing automatic on these early units and the owner had to learn how to drive them. (c) Maughan's advert from later years.

c.

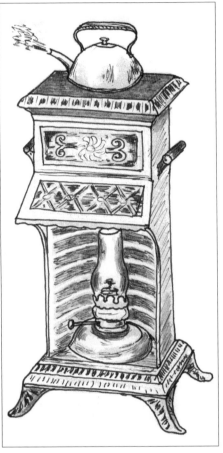

Two more household items from the second half of the 19th century. (Above) A cast-iron gas cooker produced by Fletcher Russel & Co. (Ironbridge – Blists Hill). (Right) A cast-iron heater powered by an oil lamp which probably took a long time to boil the kettle.

work, they nevertheless promoted the idea of a bathroom in every home, though this was often a converted bedroom. During this period gas rings, used to heat saucepans, appeared, followed by radiant gas fires, which like the lights still poured all their fumes into the house. During the 1870s gas cookers were developed and slowly became established in new housing where the coal-fired range was no longer welcome.

Other items of the bathroom also appeared during the 1800s such as towels, including roller towels, flannels and bath mats. Toothpaste could be purchased but for many it was still a home-made concoction of soot, ashes, honey, charcoal, areca nuts or cuttlefish bone.

It was also this period that saw the arrival of a range in the living room to heat water. This was then circulated to a hot water tank which lived on

A bedroom of the period, complete with wash stand and jug. (The Shambles)

The earliest washing machine, the 'Vowel A1', made by Thomas Bradford & Co between 1860 and 1870. (Blaise Castle Museum)

one of the higher floors, the system being fed from a cold water tank in the loft. This idea was not tried earlier as the pressure in the early pipes couldn't raise the water much above the first floor. Unfortunately, though, winters were much more severe then than those we are used to and the loft tank regularly froze. If the hot water had been drawn off (there was often a tap fitted directly to the range boiler), then when the loft thawed the sudden arrival of cold water in the dry but very hot boiler caused some dreadful explosions resulting in deaths. The plumbing industry quickly learned how to modify the boilers and the cold tank system in order to cure the problems.

The aspiring middle classes were by now becoming very fashion-conscious, not just in clothes but also in household gadgets and food preparation. Spurred on by books like Mrs Beeton's famous tome on cooking and by magazine advertising,

the wife had to have all the latest devices and utensils, including graters, lemon squeezers, whisks, steak hammers, potato mashers, colanders and sugar cutters (sugar still came in a solid cone, from which you had to break off pieces). Hand-turned devices for every possible use were made: coffee mills, marmalade

A selection of sugar cutters used to break off a lump of sugar from the sugar cone. (Milestones)

Inside an ironmonger's shop – an Aladdin's cave of fascinating items. (The Shambles)

cutters, vegetable slicers, mincing machines, meat and suet choppers, potato chippers and kitchen scales with lovely brass or iron weights.

What today we would call saucepans had developed throughout the 1800s. Cauldrons, usually cast-iron, had rounded sides and a round bottom plus three short stubby legs. These could be hung over a fire or even placed in the fire to cook. Kettles were usually made from sheet metal, were straight sided with a flat bottom and could be either hung over a fire or placed on the flat surfaces of a range to simmer away. Both of these pots had handles or loops from which they could be hung. The fixed handle that we are used to today appeared during the mid 1800s.

A portable roasting spit, which was placed against the open fire of a range. The early range ovens had very little ventilation – fine for bread baking but a disaster for roasting meat. These spits solved the problem. A clockwork motor (called a jack) slowly turned the meat, which could be checked and basted via the door. (Blaise Castle Museum)

(Above) An early pressure cooker, with an impressive clamp to retain the lid and a meter. (Milestones)

(Left) A glazed earthenware bread pan made by Doulton & Co. (Right) A coffee mill. (Blaise Castle Museum)

CHAPTER 8

Health

Though not a physical part of our domestic life, health affected every family in the land. During the 1700s and the early 1800s enormous advances had been made in understanding the human body. The various organs and the circulation of blood had been unravelled but the only area to show any benefit was surgery, always the down-to-earth branch of medicine. The causes of disease and thus the knowledge to cure them were still a mystery. Slowly, during the 1850–1900 period, the first experiments were made to identify the mechanisms, and eventually the concept of bacteria and viruses was established. This discovery turned medicine on its head. The realization that 'germs' carried illness and that this link could be broken by simply washing hands, clothing and the surroundings of the sickbed, changed hospital practices forever. Though she didn't realize the underlying reason, Florence Nightingale had long advocated cleanliness in hospitals and her success in reducing the death rates was always acknowledged at the highest level. In parallel with these discoveries experiments with chemicals and natural elements were taking place and the first drugs were appearing. It

A wonderful collection of patent medicines, including Boots Throat Pastilles, Vaseline Camphor Ice, Gees Linctus and Milk of Magnesia. (Claydon Bygones Museum)

Following on from quack medicines, food producers started to claim dietary health benefits for their factory-made products. (Milestones)

was to take many years before these breakthroughs made a real impact on life expectancy but the health revolution had started. One strange problem had been noticed – that was the recurrence of typhoid and other fever-like diseases in the middle classes but not in the poor. Though it took time to understand the problem, it came down to our poor old plumber. There were two problems associated with the plumbing in the new middle-class houses: one was the habit of venting almost everything directly into the sewer stack, the other was just plain poor workmanship in laying sewers. It is strange that, having worked to isolate the WC from the stack pipe with a water seal, all other pipes were left unprotected. The drains and overflow from the basins and baths simple joined the sewer pipe directly. Worse still, the sewer stack pipe, often in the centre of the house, vented at its top end into the loft, often near the cold water tank. This tank not only supplied the hot water system but all the cold taps in the house, i.e. the drinking water. Lucky poor people with their garden privy and one cold tap!

Depending on when a house was built, the lavatory might still be a privy at the bottom of the garden or the privy might be attached to the rear of the house. In the latter case there may even be a flushing water closet. This period also saw the invention of the earth closet by the Rev Henry Moule in 1860, an idea that has resurfaced several times since. In this, the use of earth or ash mixed with the waste was not just to reduce the smell until the night soil men carted it away but to allow natural bacterial action to digest the waste, leaving an almost smell-free compost. Modern versions gently heat the compost to achieve a much quicker digestion.

At first water closets were placed within the bedroom; they were in effect replacing the chamber pot. Later they would be fitted within a separate small room, the precursor to the modern-day bathroom. Joseph Bramah's early WC was improved during this period by companies like George Jennings, Thomas Crapper, D. T. Bostel and Thomas Twyford. By 1890 most WCs were now connected to the sewer via a water trap formed by a sharp 'S' shape in the pipe, which acted as a barrier to the smells. It was first patented in 1775 by a watchmaker named Cummings. By adopting porcelain bowls and a syphon-operated cistern, toilets that we would recognize today started to appear, though in true Victorian style the variations were endless. Another invention arrived from America around 1860 – toilet paper. Perforated toilet rolls, usually a hard thin paper, arrived in the 1880s more or less completing the development of the WC. Softer papers didn't arrive until the 1930s, which partly explains why neatly-torn sheets of newspaper threaded onto a piece of string adorned many privies into the 1950s.

The Victorians, or at least the posh ones, were incredibly prudish and things like toilet paper were never on display in a shop; it was asked for by the product brand name and discreetly passed over by the shopkeeper. Bramah had obtained permission to exhibit his flushing toilet in the Great Exhibition of 1851 but the possibility of offending was great and the idea was considered very risky indeed. When the exhibition was re-sited in Crystal Palace this item was quietly dropped!

In the cities another health risk started to appear – smog. From time to time in winter the weather conditions create fog, often in the low river valleys, just where most major cities lie. What we might find hard to

Another attempt to reduce smells in the privy and, it was believed, the risk of disease, was this device which allowed the user to deposit a layer of soil and ash over the contents of the bucket.

Highly decorated lavatory that may well have been placed within a bedroom.

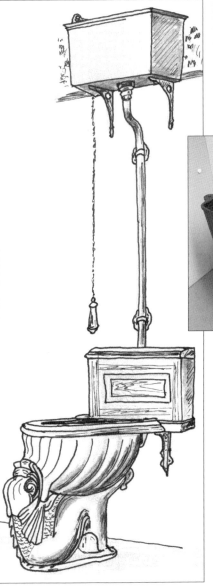

understand today is just how much sulphurous smoke is put into the air by coal fires. Rows and rows of tightly-packed terrace houses, many with more than one fire burning, all poured smoke into the fog. In addition were the many factories with their coal-burning boilers and numerous chimneys, a sight that has almost

The source of the thunderous noise when flushing a lavatory. An early cast-iron cistern using the now obsolete bell to cause the siphon to work. (Abbey Pumping Station Museum)

completely vanished from the scene today. With no way to escape, the smoke mixed with the damp fog producing an impenetrable soup of nasty-tasting smog. Even if the sun was shining above the fog layer, it would now be very dull at ground level and the mixture proved very bad for those suffering from any kind of bronchial trouble. In 1880 some 700 people died as a result of smog, a problem that recurred from time to time right up to the Clean Air Acts and smokeless fuels of the 1950s.

Classic late-Victorian WC with the extremely effective, though noisy, thunder box cistern.

It is very hard to imagine just how many chimneys there were at the end of the 19th century. This photo shows part of Nottingham on a cold day around 1900.
(Picture the Past)

Now that's what you call pollution! Widnes had quite a reputation for smoke – this picture from around 1900 shows the problem. (Liverpool Library)

CHAPTER 9

The Quiet Revolution – Electricity

As already mentioned, simple wet cell batteries had been invented in the mid 19th century and, apart from novelty uses, the first real application of electricity was the telegraph. By connecting the battery to a pair of wires which fed a detector at the far end, simple on/off signals could be sent. Improvements in the detector based on the Danish physicist Hans Christian Oerstadt's work on magnetism meant that much longer distances could be covered and, by the 1840s, links of 30 and 40 miles were in use. In 1837 Samuel Finley Breese Morse invented his system of representing letters by a dot or dash code, improved on over the years until in 1851 the International Morse Code was established and remained in use until the 1960s. (The Morse code distress code SOS was finally abandoned in 1999.)

In 1850 the English Channel was crossed by a submarine telegraph cable, which suffered the indignity of being cut through by a French fisherman on its second day of operation. Within a year armoured cable had been developed and a successful cable linked England and France. In 1858 an attempt to cross the Atlantic by cable lasted only a week but the telegraph idea was proven; it was the physical strength of the cable that had failed. Local and international communication was born and indirectly affected everyone.

From the point of view of our domestic life it was the work of Michael Faraday that brought the real changes. Following on from Oerstadt, mentioned above, Faraday developed the basic motor and electric generator in the 1830s. Like all first attempts it was inefficient and barely practical, but with the efforts of many other engineers the machines were slowly improved until, by the 1850s, steam-driven generators were being used to power arc lights in streets and theatres. Electric motors also slowly improved but had to wait for better electricity distribution methods before they became really useful.

The principle of generating electricity is fairly simple but, because neither electricity nor the magnetic fields needed to make it can be seen, it possesses a slight air of black magic. What Oerstadt had observed was that a coil of wire moved through a magnet produced a pulse of electric current. To generate electricity it needed an arrangement of coils that were continuously moving in and out of a magnetic field. Faraday realized that, if a coil could be rotated within a magnet, then the coil would experience continuous changes in the magnetic flux.

The next problem was how to get

The next step was to use massive coils to replace the magnet as here in this Wilson-Hartell dynamo which would have been turned by a steam engine. (The Waterworks Museum)

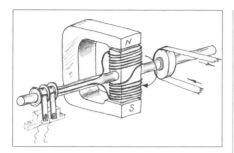

Simplified drawing showing the basic idea of generating electricity. The commutator shown here (far left) produces AC.

the electric current from the rotating coil and this was solved by the commutator. This consisted of a pair of copper sleeves to which the coil was wired and onto which rested a pair of contacts. Depending on how the commutator is arranged, one collects a series of electrical pulses going the same way – crude direct current (DC) – or the pulses alternate, first going one way and then the other – primitive alternating current (AC). By using multiple coils and some very clever magnetic systems it was soon possible to generate fairly smooth DC or the sinusoidal AC that we all use today.

In parallel with this work was the search for a successful electric light. The British chemist Humphry Davy had demonstrated in 1801 how an electric current from a battery would make a thin strip of platinum glow brightly, but, because it was in air, the metal simply burnt away in minutes. By 1848 Joseph Swan was experimenting with different types of material, trying to find one that would last longer as a filament. He had

overcome the problem of the air by putting his filaments in an evacuated glass bulb. By 1860 he had patented a carbon filament light, but it was still very short lived. In 1879 finally he was able to demonstrate a practical lamp, but the prolific American inventor Thomas Edison was also working to the same end and just 10 months after Swan's demonstration he showed his own lamps. By the following year Edison had used carbonized bamboo fibre to produce a lamp that burnt for over 1,000 hours. Both men pushed ahead. Swan was responsible for lighting Parliament and the British Museum, whilst Edison had lit the steamship *Columbia*, a New York printing company and, by 1882, had commissioned a central power station in Manhattan. Edison certainly had the commercial flair to drive his ideas, which he did brilliantly. After a short period of legal action over patents Edison and Swan formed a joint company in 1883. Edison was interested in the whole field of electricity and developed the concept

Early lamps by Swan (left) and Edison (right) from the 1890s.

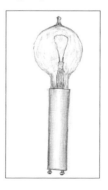

of central generators from which power was distributed to the local neighbourhood, but he had pioneered the use of direct current, the steady supply that comes from a battery.

We must now take a brief technical diversion to understand why the direct current route was doomed to fail. When passing an electric current through a cable there is a loss of power, which shows up as heat. This loss simply depends on the amount of current and how thick the cable is, so to keep the losses low over long distances requires very thick cables. One way around this is to raise the voltage which has the effect of reducing the amount of current flowing which, in turn, means smaller cable. The problem for Edison's DC system was that it is very difficult to change the voltage; so whatever voltage you choose has to stay the same from the generator, through the cables and, most important of all, into the factories and homes. Any voltage over the 100-volt mark can give a nasty shock and voltages over 200 can prove fatal, so Edison kept his systems to 110 volts. As demand grew the cables had to get bigger and it was soon realized that taking DC power over distances of more than a few miles was impractical.

Meanwhile, the American industrialist George Westinghouse had taken up the cause for the slightly more complex alternating current system, where the voltage is constantly reversing, following a smooth sine wave (alternating current or AC). This form of electricity can be easily changed from low to high voltage and back using a transformer. It was now possible to generate power at a voltage that made best use of the generators

and, using transformers, it could be sent over long distances at a high voltage (and thus low current and in thin wires) and then be transformed down to the domestic voltages, where needed. This is the principle behind our national grid and the pylons we see marching across the countryside carrying very high voltages but using relatively thin wires. Despite Edison still installing DC systems – Godalming in Surrey being the first in England in 1881, followed by Holborn and Brighton – the DC system was not to last. Filament lights will work on AC or DC and engineers soon designed motors that worked on AC as well. Strictly speaking, DC can be changed but only by the somewhat crude means of using it to drive a DC motor, which, in turn, drives another DC generator set for a different voltage. Motors and generators are moving machinery that need maintenance and care whereas the transformer is completely static and needs no attention at all.

By 1880 the English Crompton Company had been set up, making reliable AC generators based on a Swiss design, though the German Siemens Company was always at the forefront of electric generation and traction. At this point electricity was still generated locally but in 1887 the London Electric Supply Company was formed to realize an ambitious scheme devised by Ferranti. In Deptford, they built what today we would recognize as a power station. It housed two alternators producing AC electricity at 5,000 volts, driven by a 1,250 hp steam engine, plus four further alternators generating at 10,000 volts, driven by a 10,000 hp steam engine. At the time these were seriously large machines! The power

By the turn of the century seriously large alternators were in use. This Swedish-designed steam turbine machine had the turbine in the centre and two alternators at the ends. Built by the Brush Electrical Engineering Company, this unit was in use from 1914 to 1960. (Abbey Pumping Station Museum)

Drawing of a typical 1920s generating hall with several turbine-alternators plus an array of control gear.

relatively easy compared with gas, water and sewage, which all needed underground pipework. Though often installed just for lighting, the domestic appliance industries were beavering away and, by the end of the 1800s, electricity was powering the new electric trams, factories and workshops, homes and shops, plus the original use – street lighting.

The familiar transformer in a rural area changing the 6.6 kv lines (top) down to 230 v for the local village.

Notice that cast-iron is still supreme in this early electric cooker. Providing just two hotplates and an oven, each having a choice of low, medium or full. The hole in front of the left-hand hotplate is to show how the elements were made.
(Ironbridge – Blists Hill Victorian Town)

was taken into London by overhead cables and transformed down to the lower domestic voltages near to the point of usage.

In 1884 Parsons had developed the steam turbine, originally to power ships, but the naturally high rotating speed of the turbine was just what the latest alternators needed and turbines took over from reciprocating engines in all new power stations.

Electricity could be distributed to houses by stringing the cables along the streets on poles and taking a feed to each house, just as we still see in rural areas today. This made it

CHAPTER 10

The Utilities

By now all four major utility industries were established and though we probably think of water and sewerage as the first on the scene it was gas that became organized and regulated first. The British Association of Gas Engineers was formed in 1863, to be followed by the Institution of Municipal Engineers in 1873 and, in a late flurry, Sanitation, Water Supply, and Heating & Ventilation in 1895, 1896 and 1897 respectively. This period saw steady advances made in all the utility works.

Water was now often pumped using

A restored triple expansion engine that pumped the water in the Hereford Water Works, erected in 1893. One set of pumps sent water from the river Wye up the hill to the treatment ponds, which then returned it to a second pump which pumped it up to the distribution tower. (The Waterworks Museum)

triple expansion steam engines. Originally developed for ships, these machines use the steam in three stages, extracting every last bit of energy from it. The end result was greater efficiency plus greater power outputs as more and more water was demanded by both home and industry.

Water treatment now involved passing the water from the reservoir through sand and charcoal beds which removed most particles but still not the bacteria. With the isolation of sewage, most river and bore hole sources were fairly bacteria-free and, providing the filtered water was kept covered, it was pretty good. The biggest challenge was keeping up with the vast increase in the quantity needed. Massive reservoir systems sprang up along large rivers like the Thames and Trent, and boring down into water-bearing strata increased ten-fold. To give an idea of the numbers, the modest-sized city of Leicester in 1850 already had around 3,000 public wells, bore holes and pumps.

Manchester revived the idea of bringing water from sources many miles away when around 1900 the 70-mile-long Thirlmere aqueduct from the Lake District was built. Today, this brings nearly 50 million gallons of water every day to the Manchester ring main. Birmingham and Liverpool use similar systems to bring water from Wales.

Hereford's water distribution tower built in 1883 to hold 45,000 gallons of water. Today this tower would hold enough water to supply Hereford for just four minutes!

Rather than just dumping raw sewage, methods of treatment had now been developed whereby the organic nature of the waste was made use of by allowing helpful bacteria to break down the material into virtually clean water and a harmless sludge that could be dried and which formed the basis of many popular fertilizer products.

Progress had also been made in the general municipal area of household waste disposal, the first destructor (incinerator) having been erected in Ealing, west of London, in 1883. These early units could not sustain the 1,250°F that is needed to destroy everything, however, and they gave off an unpleasant smoke. This was tackled by an add-on device called a 'fume cremator' that attempted to clean up the smoke. Eventually, in the 1890s, using a forced air draught and coke as fuel, the necessary temperatures were reached and the incinerator became established.

The gas industry, though still local, continued to improve. A steady flow of technical inventions provided for cleaner gas and better separation of the by-products. The retorts now had doors at each end, allowing the red hot coke to be pushed out at the end of a burn – the men no longer had to rake the coke towards themselves. In the 1880s inclined retorts had been developed, allowing the coke to be simply dropped out of the lower end and then recharged with coal poured in at the top end. In 1870 the Gas, Light and Coke Company opened the world's largest gas works at Beckton. This sent its gas to London in a 48-inch diameter pipe, with a smaller extension to Westminster. There were 10 single lift gas holders, as the Thames estuary was considered too windy for anything taller. At its peak it was employing some 2,000 people and producing 25 million cubic feet of gas every day. In time a second similar pipe was added to cope with the increased demand and the gas was now being pumped along the pipes to achieve a better flow. In 1888 large spiral-guided gas holders were introduced, including a mammoth 12½ million cubic feet gas holder erected in Greenwich which had six sections or lifts but was eventually destroyed in the Second World War.

By 1891 there were 600 gas companies at work, supplying around 2.3 million customers via some 22,000 miles of gas mains. This immense increase in usage is reflected in the home where the installation of gas cookers rose from a modest 7,000 in 1892 to over 36,000 just four years later. These were still called 'kitcheners', inheriting the name from the coal-fired range cookers. Gas was replacing coal in industry as well, finding use in pottery, glass, heat treatment of metals and the making of the glass light bulbs for its rival industry – electricity. One unexpected change was in the baking of bread. In 1880 there were around 60,000 bakeries facing constant complaints of contamination in the bread and of smoke from the ovens. Gas fired ovens solved these problems at a stroke, and slowly the entire industry changed over to gas. To spread its use in the home, gas showrooms were opened and cookers could be hired. To encourage working class folk to move over to gas, the connection charge was dropped but a higher price was charged for the gas, paid for by the use of coin-in-the-slot pre-payment meters introduced in 1887.

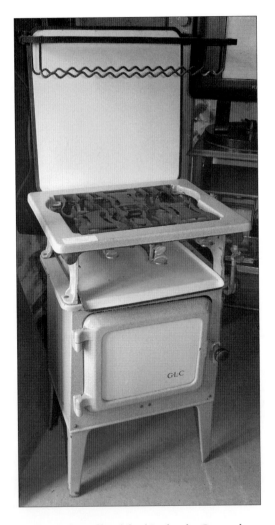

A gas cooker offered for hire by the Gas and Light Company. These cookers were designed and made by the traditional manufacturing companies and supplied to the G&L Co. (Fakenham Museum of Gas)

SECTION
III

1900 – 1950

CHAPTER 11

Change is Afoot

It is always difficult to view the 20th century realistically. Firstly, the very name '20th' sounds so much more modern than 18th or 19th. It is also the century that saw possibly the greatest changes so far to our domestic lives.

Towards the end of the 19th century there had been a series of disastrous years in agriculture owing to appalling weather. The year 1879 had been the wettest on record, with outbreaks of foot and mouth disease, plus liver-rot in sheep. In the same period the mass production of wheat in the Americas and of meat in Australia and New Zealand reached a zenith. The stab in the back for the UK farmer was the arrival at the same time of reliable steam ships and bulk refrigeration. The new cheap food now arrived in vast quantities, and the value of agricultural land crashed. Grain prices dropped by some 60 per cent between 1877 and 1894, and a loaf which cost 10 pence in the 1870s was below 6 pence in the early 1900s. The landed gentry lost millions, the first of many blows that were to rock our traditional social order.

In our society there had always been a so-called middle class: lawyers, doctors, accountants, and the more skilled artisans. Before the Industrial Revolution they had formed a very small group totally dependent on the rich who employed them. During the 1800s this group expanded rapidly as knowledge and organizational skills became more and more important, until, by 1900, the middle classes, now some 15 per cent of the population, were indispensable. Landowners or not, the country could not run without the middle classes and they knew it! There was a fundamental shift in the centuries-old structure of our country.

At the start of the 20th century it was estimated that there were 1.5 million women in service but, just as the agricultural workers had left their traditional poorly paid jobs on the land, so now did the mass of single women leave domestic service. It had been one of the only employment opportunities for females, but now industry and business offered better money and better conditions. This put more wealth into a stratum of society that was vibrant and looking for a better life. With fewer servants and maids, the upper classes needed a more efficient environment at home, and ladies now earning their own money expected a less mundane lifestyle. The balance of the government changed and so did attitudes. One result was a boom in house building, not just quantity but new styles.

As always there was a gradient from the manual worker right up to the top of the middle class but this period saw an upward shift right across the board. Massive networks of trams and suburban railways enabled people to travel to work, as indeed did the

Two examples of outside gas lighting: the first a simple street light which could be turned on and off by the lamp lighter, a job still going well into the 1950s. The example below has a clockwork timer and battery ignition unit which enabled it to run unattended for days. (Fakenham Museum of Gas)

arrival of the safety bicycle in 1883. One could now live on the outskirts of town and still reach the traditional working areas. Masses of old slum buildings were cleared and, in the biggest boom in building ever, suburbia was born. Virtually all the new housing, however humble, had clean water, mains sewerage and gas for lighting and heating. Many had the new electricity as well. At this point all four utilities were still local with every town or city having its own water, gas, sewage and electricity works. Coal was now consumed in enormous quantities, both domestically via the coal merchant who operated from every large railway station, and also in factories.

Outside, gas lighting hung on longer than one might have expected, particularly in streets and railway stations, but slowly the electric light replaced it. The car had now arrived and by 1929 there were over one million cars in Britain, and the same year saw over 300,000 motor lorries registered. The cost of a small car dropped from around £500 in 1920 to just £125 by 1930. The horse was now rapidly vanishing from the big towns and cities and with it a vast network of farriers, stables and foodstuff suppliers.

The first 50 years of the 20th century were to see changes that even the Victorians would have found alarming. Trade unions slowly broke down the take-it-or-leave-it attitudes of employers, National Insurance (1909) offered the first thin line of security – pensions for the over 70s. Schooling became compulsory up to the age of 14, when children were expected to start work. In 1900 the American, Charles Coudler, introduced us to Coca Cola. Aspirin went on sale in 1905, joining a well-established list of less effective quack medicines. In 1911 the Shops Act gave all workers the right to a half-day holiday every week which, for most in industry or commerce, meant having Saturday afternoons off. This massive release of people now able to spend time on pleasure kick-started the following of sports, in particular, football. Aeroplanes, the wireless, the gramophone and telephones kept the thrust of invention in the public eye. Alas, it was all disrupted by the two largest wars the planet has ever seen, but even these sad events pushed social changes and technology onwards ever faster.

Bathroom from the early 1900s, complete with torn newspaper rather than harsh Bronco. Note how it has been squeezed under a staircase and is still gas lit. (Black Country Living Museum)

The kitchen might have an electric cooker and copper, whilst a stand-alone coal boiler would warm the room and supply hot water.

The new homes changed in just two areas: the kitchen and the bathroom. These now combined what had been a miscellany of functions. Food storage, preparation and cooking joined the old scullery function of laundry in a single room – the kitchen. The typical house now had two other ground floor rooms, the living room or dining room and the parlour or front room reserved for special events and best behaviour. Both would have coal fireplaces and often the living room fire would have a rear boiler to provide the house with hot water. A popular alternative was to have a small coal boiler in the kitchen. The bathroom at last acknowledged the basic pleasure of washing and bathing, with these functions leaving the bedrooms and kitchens. This was joined by the lavatory though this was sometimes allotted a separate small room adjacent to the bathroom. Now relieved of the functional aspects of life, the remaining living rooms and bedrooms could take on a lighter and more fashionable decor. Bedrooms were often provided with small fireplaces but these were rarely lit unless someone was ill. Blankets and a ceramic hot water bottle were still

Electrical appliances grew apace. Left is a smart portable fire and below an electric heater for hair tongs and above another popular portable fire from around 1930. (Blaise Castle Museum and Think Tank)

the defence against the winter cold.

As is so often the case in a new phase of life, there was nothing actually new; what had changed was the scale. Though of every possible architectural style, these basic modern houses were built in vast numbers and usually to a high standard, indeed they are still housing millions of us today.

Fashion and skilful marketing drove a wonderful array of styles which swept through our homes, aided by developments in the manufacture of appliances. The Ideal Home Exhibition,

An old rotary knife cleaner. The blades would be inserted into the slots along the top and an abrasive polishing wheel inside would clean the ever-rusting steel.
(Cogges Manor Farm Museum)

A Thor washing machine, complete with motor driven wringer. (Blaise Castle Museum)

A Jackson cooker which made good use of enamelling. (Blaise Castle Museum)

A gas-heated iron showing the use of enamelling to make a more attractive finish. These heated up quickly but unfortunately the whole iron would get too hot, making it difficult to use. (Think Tank)

A radiant gas fire ready to be set into an old fireplace where the chimney would take away the fumes. (Milestones)

that wonderful collection of ideas, marketing and gadget salesmen, started in 1920 and continues to this day.

In 1913 stainless steel arrived, heralding the end of cleaning cutlery. The same year saw the arrival of the zip fastener from Sweden. Sheet steel started to replace cast-iron in the 1920s, with new, lighter cookers, fires and baths. Enamel (the substance being more akin to glass than paint) provided tough clean surfaces. Enamelling, in fact, is quite clever, having the same heat expansion characteristics as steel. Baths could get very hot and both the bath and the enamel coating expanded together, thus preventing cracking. This made

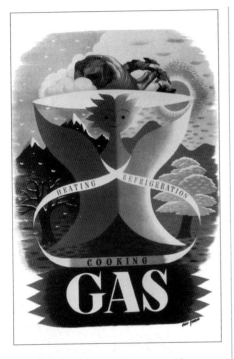

(Above) the original Mr Therm, drawn by Eric Frazer, and (below) one of the more modern incarnations.

A delightful advertisement by the 'Main' company for gas cooking.

enamel the ideal surface for gas heaters, saucepans and cookers.

In 1909 tungsten was introduced for the filaments in electric light bulbs, giving a brighter element and a whiter light. Indeed, heavy lampshades became popular in order to reduce the glare of these lights. It was this change that really set the move against gas lighting with its attendant smell and dirty ceilings. Electricity was also physically easier to apply to small appliances and soon it replaced gas for items like hair curlers, irons, and small portable heaters. Heating elements had originally been made with iron wire but this suffered from rusting, a problem solved by the development of nichrome (a mixture of nickel and chrome). In 1912 C. R. Belling wound nichrome wire around fire clay strips and so was born the familiar heating element. Surprisingly it wasn't a requirement for electric fires to have guards until 1952 but, of course, this was the era of open coal fires – everyone understood the dangers.

The gas industry responded with a vigorous advertising campaign aided from 1933 by 'Mr Therm' promoting domestic appliances such as water heaters and cookers. The regulo thermostat for automatically controlling the temperature of the gas oven appeared in 1924. Those who could afford it would now have a refrigerator, which could be either gas or electric.

The coal fire still reigned supreme for heating the house and usually the hot water as well, though gas geysers were becoming more common in bathrooms and kitchens. Most fireplaces had a gas tap adjacent, which could be used for a gas fire or, as I remember well, for a gas poker to light the coal fire instead of having to use paper and wood to get the coal going.

Gas cookers were still cast-iron in the 1920s, when this New Main example was made. (Blaise Castle Museum)

An early gas refrigerator made by Electrolux, who still produce gas fridges for the caravan and boating industries. (Fakenham Museum of Gas)

household plants soon died, all that is except one tough plant that was to become almost the symbol of Edwardian life – the aspidistra.

In rural areas the arrival of electricity was a major turning point. It meant the end of candles for lighting, ceilings now stayed clean and needlework was possible in the evenings without eye strain. Though many decades behind the large towns and cities, running water and proper sewers were now reaching more rural areas.

A Duplex gas radiator in beautiful deep green enamel. (Blaise Castle Museum)

The classic Edwardian scene, the piano and in the corner an aspidistra. (Black Country Living Museum)

There was an alarming disregard for safety in some of the gas products, including several full-sized cookers that were intended to be fed via a rubber tube from a gas tap or even from a gas light fitting. One side effect of all the gas burning was that

A last farewell to gas as a means of lighting the home. (The Shambles)

Gas held the trump card in heating water quickly, the job of the gas geyser. Examples by Lide, Ascot and Main. (Fakenham Museum of Gas)

A Shanks bath complete with shower. These free-standing baths have now come back into fashion.

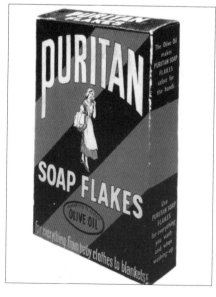

Soap flakes from early in the 1900s. (Persil arrived in 1909). (Blaise Castle Museum)

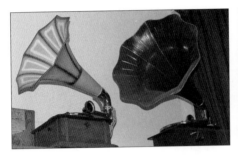

A last farewell to the delightful objects of the 1930s. Two lovely examples of the old acoustic gramophone which, like the portable version on the right, would have played 10 or 12 inch 78 rpm records. (Milestones)

(Below) A Kodak camera from the 1920s and (below right) a manually operated vacuum cleaner from 1910 – lucky maids! (Milestones)

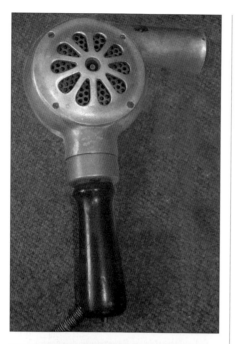

(Top left) A hair dryer; (top right) three versions of the best selling Hoover Junior dating from 1926 to 1946. This cleaner out-sold all others; (left) an early electric iron – no temperature control, just on or off; (right) an early toaster. (Milestones)

CHAPTER 12

Science Marches On

By the 1930s radios all ran on mains electricity. Using valves, they took time to warm up and work. Tuning the station involved moving a pointer along a dial. (Avoncroft Museum of Historic Buildings)

The radio, or wireless as it was known, had been established in the 1920s but most early sets would have run on accumulators, which had to be taken to the local hardware store to be recharged. Once the mains arrived this chore vanished. The well-off would also have a telephone at home, whilst the rest of us had the public telephone box, the first being erected in Egham in Surrey in 1919. All would involve an operator who worked in the local telephone exchange. When you lifted the receiver, the operator would ask which number you required and would connect you via a network of similar operators to your number. If you received a call it would be the operator who would ring you to let you know. By the mid 1930s telephones with dials appeared, along with the automatic exchange, but this was still limited to your local area only. Even in the 1950s you still needed the operator to make a long-distance or overseas call.

Home entertainment in these pre-TV days involved a wide range of simple pastimes. Mother might well do mending, embroidery or make clothes for the children or produce rugs from old material. Stamp and card collecting were very popular, as was reading, aided by public libraries, which were springing up everywhere. Magazines were eagerly awaited as were the comics for the children. Shops often hired out books for a small fee, including Boots the Chemist, which ran a substantial 'Book Lovers' subscription library service. Jigsaws, games like snakes and ladders and ludo, or simply doing the crossword in the daily paper all combined with the occasional sing-song around the piano or gramophone to fill one's leisure time.

The rich really had few things that the middle classes didn't possess – just better versions. Their motor car would be large and plush, the refrigerator bigger, the servants would still toil with the coal and there would be carpets rather than lino on the floors

(linoleum was a layer of compressed cork, sawdust, oil and glue, bound to a canvas backing which could be printed to give an attractive waterproof finish, a precursor of vinyl). The upper classes may well have enjoyed the luxury of air travel. A scheduled service began running from London to Paris in 1919 and Imperial Airways was launched in 1924. The one thing they alone might have had was the newfangled television, which started in 1936.

A phone from the 1940s, with the dial showing letters and numbers. The number you dialled would start with three letters representing the exchange you were calling. (Bewdley Museum)

Away from the kitchen, coal fires were still standard. Highly-decorated Edwardian examples were prized and kept in beautiful condition.

A modified K1 telephone box from around 1928. It was made from reinforced concrete with a wooden door and was extensively used in rural areas. (Avoncroft Museum of Historic Buildings)

The set was very expensive, very large, the screen very small and the picture was coarse and in black and white.

One other aspect of life that might surprise us today was the number of trades that plied their wares in the streets of the towns and cities. Foodstuffs like milk, bread and fish were sold from carts or vans, as were vegetables. Other callers offered brushes and household nick-nacks or a knife sharpening service. Shears and lawn mowers would be taken

The electric motor spread to all manner of appliances and very soon the food mixer took on this basic layout, made by many different companies. (Milestones)

The first electric refrigerators often had the compressor mounted on top of the cabinet giving this somewhat odd appearance. (Milestones)

Early television sets were combined with the radio you needed to receive the sound, which was transmitted separately on the medium wave. This HMV set from 1936 originally cost £36.

and returned the following week, duly sharpened or repaired.

One last domestic invention which just scrapes into our pre-1950 time frame is the microwave oven. Microwaves are extremely high-frequency electromagnetic waves produced by a device called a magnetron, developed in Britain during the Second World War for use in radar. Their use for heating was realized but ignored until Dr Percy

Spencer, who was working in the USA on radar developments, noticed a slightly melted peanut bar in his pocket. He quickly realized that it was due to microwave radiation. Intrigued, he cooked an egg in a kettle onto which he had fitted a magnetron, cooked isn't really the word, the egg exploded! The research was taken up by the Raytheon Company, who filed a patent in 1946. The first commercial microwave ovens were marketed in 1947 for the modest sum of £30,000! Domestic versions following during the next decade but again were still very costly.

A microwave oven called the Microrange, from the 1960s. Most early machines only had a power rating in the 400 to 500 watt range.

CHAPTER 13

Into the 1950s

The still-familiar sight of rotating sprinklers over filter beds. These serve the Droitwich area.

⬚ WATER

Two factors continued to change in the water industry: coping with the ever increasing demand and improving the quality. There was a major step forward in the filtering, whereby sand and gravel were still used to filter out the solid matter but now chemicals were being used to remove bacteria. Chlorine, pumped through the water in gas form, was the main weapon in this period. Extracting water from both bore-holes and rivers was slowly taken over by electric pumps, as was the raising of the water to the local tower or elevated covered reservoir. Something that is easy to forget is that all domestic cold water piping was made of lead at this time. Extremely malleable and easy to repair or alter, it was produced in vast quantities. Iron pipework was used for hot water or anywhere that involved high pressures.

⬚ SEWAGE

The treatment of sewage also underwent a change, at least in sites away from the sea. After mechanical removal of all manner of strange objects, including bricks, rags and dead animals, bacteria were introduced to break down the waste into liquid and sludge. The sludge was

The modern treatment works at Crossness. At the top end of the site is the preserved pump house from Bazalgette's day. The building nearest the camera is the power plant which burns the dried sludge, producing nearly all the electricity the site needs. The old storage tanks seen on page 51 were under the ground to the left of the pump house. (Thames Water)

Undeniably ugly, this modern exercise in concrete supplies the Droitwich area with water. These structures also make ideal platforms for telecommunication dishes and radio aerials.

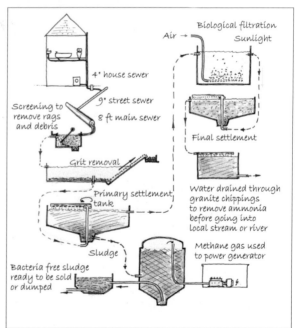

Diagram showing the story of typical sewage treatment. Starting from our homes, the waste goes through the sewage works to finally leave as pure water and usable sludge.

Basic filter beds using sand and charcoal. These suffered from being relatively slow and, with the relentless increase in demand, another system had to be found.

further treated and compressed, after which it was sold as fertilizer, buried or taken out to sea. The liquids were filtered in the familiar rotating sprinkler beds and finally the ammonia was filtered out, after which the liquid was safe to pass into the local river or stream.

Towns with access to the sea still pumped the untreated sewage out to sea via long cast-iron pipes that alas didn't go that far away from the shore line. At the end of our period the methane gas from the bacteria treatment was being collected and burnt on site to provide heat and later to generate electricity. This treatment sequence is viable in quite small volumes and even modest sized villages could justify their own small sewage treatment plant. For smaller quantities still, as might come from a single farm or large house, the Klargester tank was developed, in which bacteria break down the waste before it is allowed into a local stream or river.

Enter the pressure vessel: these pressure tanks were three-quarters full of fine sand, and the water was forced through under pressure, thus speeding up the process. Each day they were back-washed to remove debris and dirt. Installed in 1931, they worked until the 1980s. Note we are no longer outdoors. (Abbey Pumping Station Museum)

⚅ GAS

The gas industry had seen a steady flow of improvements to the efficiency of their process and to the cleaning of the gas itself. Vertical retorts had been developed in which the coal was loaded at the top and steadily worked its way down whilst being 'cooked'. By the time it reached the bottom it was pure coke, the process now being continuous rather than the hectic loading and unloading of all the material in a retort every eight hours or so. More important still was the growing application of the various by-products. The chemical industries, which had their birth in the 1800s using the waste products from making coal gas, were now expanding fast and consumed all the by-products they could get. Ammoniacal liquor was used to produce explosives, refrigerants and pure ammonia; sulphur produced sulphuric acid, used in car batteries and, along with ammonia, went into many fertilizers. The tar could be broken down into an amazing range of chemicals which ended up in plastics, mothballs, vitamins, medicines and saccharin. Explosives, perfumes, photographic products, preservatives and insecticides, paints, dyes, and nylon all contained the by-products of tar.

Slowly, the local works closed as larger gas works took over the job of producing the gas and pumping it to the gas holders, which were still needed to supply the ups and downs in demand.

⊞ ELECTRICITY

The national grid was started in the 1930s and slowly the local generating stations became obsolete as large power stations were built in places where coal and water were found. It is much cheaper to move electricity around than to move millions of tons of coal and water. The grid carries electricity at 400,000 volts, transformed down to 132,000 volts for regional distribution. This in turn is taken down for industrial use and finally reduced to 415 or 240 volts for local industry and home use. (Today, our home voltage is nominally 230 volts.) Safety at home was still not quite what it might have been and it was alarmingly easy to touch live mains. In particular, light switches had a twist on cover which was easily removed leaving live parts unprotected. Many fuse boxes and plugs had a similar potential for trouble.

Bringing electricity to the rural areas relied entirely on the relatively cheap system of overhead cables and transformers, though it is subject to disruption in times of high winds or snow. The thought of living without electricity is quite horrendous to us today.

Fuses and light switches of the time. All could be opened without any trouble or tools!

CHAPTER 14

Technology Arrives

L argely propelled by the technology of the Second World War almost everything in the home saw amazing advances in production methods which had the effect of making products cheaper and smaller. New synthetic fibres led to mass produced carpets and furnishings,

The post-war 'prefab'. Erected in just four hours, it offered sumptuous living conditions to thousands of families who had lost their cramped and damp slum housing in the war. (Avoncroft Museum of Historic Buildings)

Trams had a very good life, providing public transport from the 1860s to 1962, when Glasgow finally said goodbye. (National Tramway Museum)

which, whilst not a challenge to the very best quality items, still provided the less well off with luxuries their parents couldn't have dreamt of. Kitchen appliances like food mixers, kettles and irons started to take on a lighter, more stylish look. The wash tub and mangle began to disappear as electric washing machines and spin dryers became everyday items to which most people could aspire. The microwave evolved quickly with the first affordable domestic models appearing in the 1970s. Copper

pipework and cheap pressed-steel radiators heralded the start of home central heating and the end of lead water pipes.

Cars became relatively cheap and were no longer a luxury item. Trams slowly vanished, as did the electric trolley buses, once the diesel bus became universal. Building standards now included the cavity wall, giving in turn easier heating of houses. The housing problem in the aftermath of the Second World War had given rise to the 'prefab', single storey houses that were mass-produced in factories, assembled on site in just a few days, and were dearly loved by most of those who lived in them. Designed to last for ten years, many were still in use over 40 years later, with a few still in use today. Tower flats were the other answer but they must rank as one of man's worst ideas ever! To prevent problems with high winds rushing between the towers they had to be built widely spaced and, in fact, they used as much land as conventional housing but inflicted a lonely, unsociable life on the occupants. Inside our homes there were changes that would probably alarm the Victorians – light colours, plain surfaces, emulsion paint and, heaven help us, 'Do It Yourself' decorating.

Despite this, our homes still operated as before: clean drinking water, simple reliable toilets, gas and electricity to provide heat and light, with coal still well entrenched for heating, though by 1990 it was gone, replaced by North Sea gas.

Technology enabled some truly wonderful improvements to long-established items. Colour televisions arrived, the CD replaced the gramophone record and the tape recorder, mobile telephones released us from the cable going into the wall. The personal computer, with that masterpiece of marketing over substance, 'Windows', and its somewhat more useful development, the Internet, became an apparently vital part of our lives.

Today our water comes from a vast network of reservoirs and treatment works, interconnected by hundreds of miles of pipe work. Most large cities have virtual ring mains to deliver the water and, in London, one of the best-kept secrets is the deep level water ring main. Buried 130 ft below the surface, this 8 ft diameter pipe, 51 miles long, circles London, connecting the treatment works to the 12 outlets which take the water back up to the distribution points – a massive undertaking built very quietly as the only practical way of supplying the increasing demands. Today, beneath our roads, water and gas distribution has become the province of the plastic pipe, often threaded through old and leaking iron pipes. Able to operate at a higher pressure than the old iron pipes, it can pass greater quantities of gas or water.

Virtually everything we take for granted today is simply a development of appliances and household items our grandparents would have heard of, even if they hadn't been able to afford them. In a way this last point is probably the key to the real change that the 20th century brought: now the vast majority of the population had all the trimmings that make life hectic but pleasant and healthy.

One of the most iconic designs ever, this Bush transistor radio shape is still available today.

Rugeley power station in Staffordshire is one of only a few smaller sites still generating. Until the 1960s there was a coal mine right next door but following its closure coal is now brought in by rail.

A 14 inch TV made by Stella. In the 1950s and 60s rather ugly magnifying glasses were made which fixed over the small screens to make the picture appear bigger. It was the Coronation in 1953 which kick started television in the home, after which it never looked back. (Milestones)

Timperley Treatment Works along with two large reservoirs, nestles quietly in the Severn valley. Today the water is treated with sulphuric acid and lime, which is filtered out before a small amount of chlorine is added to keep the water clean on its journey through miles of pipes to our taps.

⬛ CONCLUSION

Our journey from 1750 to 1950 may have only been 200 years long but what an incredible 200 years it was. Life probably changed more in this one period that at any time before. In transport, always a measure of a society's progress, we went from canals, to railways, to diesel and petrol powered vehicles and lastly to aeroplanes – each step making life a little faster, a little more hurried. The Industrial Revolution provided the idea of the factory, where time ruled life, and gave us new materials with which to make our products. By the end of Victoria's reign we saw massive social changes, with the newly emerging middle classes becoming ever more important and the landed gentry shrinking in the face of change. Probably the biggest social changes came as a result of the two world wars which, like a forest fire, destroyed so much but set the scene for fresh and new ideas.

Throughout this story the four major utilities were born and quietly changed so much of our domestic life. Water and sewage treatment started the health revolution and gas and electricity gave us distributable energy, which today underlines so much of our lives.

Try and imagine your home without clean running water at the taps, without a safe toilet which causes no problems or smells. Now turn off the gas supply and then turn off the electricity. At first it is difficult to imagine if we could even survive! This frightening thought can be allayed, however, by visiting one of the many museums that recreate Georgian or early Victorian life. Here we find water provided by a hand pump, the lavatory is a privy down the garden path and oil lamps or candles provide light. Energy to turn things, move loads or plough the fields comes from human toil aided by the horse or mule. Though not what we would choose, life nevertheless continued and thrived.

In these days of environmental awareness maybe we should remember just how extravagant we have become. It is our distance from where these products are made that encourages us to forget that these are natural materials that have been manipulated and supplied silently to our homes. I hope that this book will have helped to put you a little closer to these precious resources and helped to put our own modern lives into perspective.

SECTION
IV

APPENDICES

GLOSSARY

Accumulator   Early name for an acid battery.
Alternator   Rotating machine that generates AC electricity.
Back-to-back   Victorian houses where the back of one house forms the back of another but with no interconnection.
Beeswax   Yellow substance excreted by bees, used in candles and as a polish.
Blacksmith   Man who works in iron.
Cesspit   Hole, sometimes brick-lined, dug to hold human waste.
Chamber pot   Bowl, usually china, kept in the bedroom to use instead of the toilet.
Chlorine   Chemical used in very weak quantities to purify water.
Coke   Coal which has been reduced to almost pure carbon.
Current   The quantity of electricity flowing.
Cut-throat   An early type of razor with a long open blade.
Damper   Device used to control the amount of air drawn through a fire.
Destructor   Machine used to burn rubbish.
Douters   Modified scissors used to extinguish a burning candle.
Enamel   Glass-like protective coating which resists high temperatures.
Epidemic   Widespread outbreak of a disease through a community.
Exhauster   Name used in the gas industry for a pump.
Filament   The fine wire which radiates light in a light bulb.
Filter bed   A pool containing a layer of sand or gravel through which water is passed to remove dirt and other particles.
Fire brick   Type of brick used to line furnaces.
Fire clay   Special mix of clay that can be used as a weak cement in furnaces.
Gas ring   A gas burner arranged in the form of a ring.
Gasometer   A device for measuring the quantity of gas passing along a pipe.
Generator   Rotating machine to produce electricity.
Geyser   Vertical gas-fired water heater.
Gin (horse etc)   A circular track around which a horse or donkey walks, usually driving a water pump.
Glaze   A hard glass-like surface fired onto pottery.
Grate   Iron structure to contain a wood or coal fire.
Incinerator   Modern term for a destructor.
Kitchener   Name given to a coal-fired cooking range.
Leat   Artificial stream cut to divert water, usually to a mill.
Linoleum   A rather brittle floor covering, the precursor of vinyl.
Luminescent   Giving off a bright light.
Mantle   In gas lighting, a frail cover of material soaked in luminescent chemicals.
Miasma   An infectious or noxious smell.
Mothball   A ball of material soaked in camphor, used to repel moths in wardrobes.
Night soil   Euphemism for human waste which was removed by cart at night.
Pressure cooker   Saucepan which cooks at high temperatures under pressure.
Privy   Crude toilet where the waste is held in a bucket or a cesspit.
Rakers   Men who were employed to keep ditches and streams free of waste.

Range	Cooker, usually of cast iron, where the fire heats an oven and, often water too.
Razor	Sharp blade used to remove facial hair.
Register	Alternative name for a fire damper.
Reservoir	Lake holding water for distribution.
Retort	A container used to heat substances where the gases given off can be collected.
Saccharin	An artificial sweetener.
Scullery	Room used to do washing and cleaning work.
Slum	General name for an area of very crowded and poor quality housing.
Small beer	A low alcohol drink.
Smog	Dense choking fog caused by smoke and fog mixing.
Snuffers	Modified scissors used to trim the burning wick of a candle.
Soot	Sticky carbon waste produced by burning coal.
Stack pipe	A rising pipe connected to the sewers.
Stoneware	Heavy kind of pottery, often glazed.
Siphon	Pipe shaped to allow air pressure to push fluids upwards before dropping to a lower level.
Tallow	Pure form of animal fat, used in early candles.
Tar	Thick dark liquid distilled from coal.
Telegraph	Early system of sending signals over a pair of wires.
Tram	Cross between a bus and a railway coach.
Transformer	Device to change the voltage of AC electricity.
Trolley bus	Bus which used electric motors supplied by overhead wires.
Turbine	Enclosed fan turned by water or steam to produce rotating power.
Washer	In gas production, the stage at which impurities are washed out of the gas.
Water closet	Early name for a toilet.
Water trap	An 'S' shaped pipe which retains water, preventing air from passing through.
Wet battery	Battery which uses acid in liquid form, like a car battery.
Wick	A string-like thread used in candles to provide a flame.

SITES TO VISIT

B ear in mind that these sites vary in size, some are national institutions, open almost every day, some are small, volunteer-operated and only open one day a week. I strongly recommend either checking the website or telephoning before setting out to visit, to confirm opening times and costs.

Specialist Museums

ABBEY PUMPING STATION MUSEUM, Corporation Rd, Leicester. Tel. 0116 2995111 www.leicester.gov. uk/museums *Excellent museum of water and sewerage plus two massive beam engines (sometimes working).*

AVONCROFT MUSEUM OF HISTORIC BUILDINGS, Bromsgrove, Worcs. Tel. 01527 831363 www.avoncroft.org.uk

Abbey Pumping Statiom

BLAISE CASTLE MUSEUM, Henbury, Bristol. Tel. 0117 9039818 www.bristol.gov.uk/ccm/content/ leisure-culture/museums-galleries/bristol-blaise-castle-house-museum *Exellent small museum with lovely collection of domestic fixtures.*

CLAYDON BYGONES MUSEUM, near Banbury, Oxford. *Small rural museum with a wide selection of items on show.*

GEFFRYE MUSEUM, Kingsland Rd, London E2. Tel. 020 77399893 www.geffrye-museum.org.uk *Delightful range of period rooms set out in 18th century almshouses, featuring middle class living rooms, with emphasis on furniture and textiles.*

Geffrye Museum – photographed by Morley von Sternberg

FAKENHAM MUSEUM OF GAS, Hempton Rd, Fakenham, Norfolk. Tel. 01328 863150 www.northnorfolk.org/fakenhammuseum *Unique small gas works (non working), very helpful volunteer staff. Currently only opens on Thursdays and bank holidays.*

KEW BRIDGE STEAM MUSEUM, Green Dragon Lane, Brentford, Middlsex. Tel. 020 856 84757 *Two of the oldest and largest preserved beam engine water pumps in the world.*

Fakenham Gas Works

PAPPLEWICK PUMPING STATION, Longdale Lane, Ravenshead, Nottingham. Tel. 0115 9632938 www.papplewickpumpingstation.co.uk *Two beam-engine-driven water pumps.*

THE WATERWORKS MUSEUM, Broomy Hill, Hereford. Tel. 01432 357236 www.waterworksmuseum.org.uk *Busy museum featuring the story of water.*

Papplewick Pumps

Victorian Museums

THE BLACK COUNTRY LIVING MUSEUM, Tipton Rd, Dudley, West Midlands. Tel. 0121 5579643 www.bclm.co.uk *Popular museum featuring all things late Victorian/Edwardian, with plenty of live demonstrations.*

COGGES MANOR FARM MUSEUM, Witney, Oxford. Tel. 01993 772602 www.oxfordshire.gov.uk *Biased towards farming but with a superb restored house.*

Hereford Water Works

IRONBRIDGE – Blists Hill Victorian Town, Telford, Shropshire. Tel. 01952 884391 www.ironbridge.org.uk *Another massive complex, spread over 7 sites. Blists Hill is one of the best places to see recreated Victorian activities.*

MILESTONES, Churchill Way West, Basingstoke, Hampshire. Tel. 01256 477766 www.milestones-museum.com *Delightful museum covering the 1850 to 1950 period.*

Black Country Museum

THE NORTH OF ENGLAND OPEN AIR MUSEUM, Beamish, County Durham. Tel. 0191 3704000 www.beamish.org.uk *Massive site, features shops and house from around 1913.*

THE SHAMBLES, Church St, Newent, Glos. Tel. 01531 822144 *Reconstruction of a small Victorian town with amazing collection of artefacts.*

Cogges Manor Farm

CASTLE MUSEUM, Eye of York, York. Tel. 01904 687687 www.yorkcastlemuseum.org.uk *Takes the story right up to the 1950s.*

The Shambles

General Museums

ABBEY HOUSE MUSEUM, Kirkstall, Leeds.
Tel. 0113 2305492 www.leeds.gov.uk/abbeyhouse

BEWDLEY MUSEUM, Worcestershire.
Tel. 01299 403573

CASTLE MUSEUM, Eye of York, York.
Tel. 01904 687687 www.yorkcastlemuseum.org.uk

MUSEUM OF SCIENCE AND TECHNOLOGY
(MOSI), Liverpool Rd, Castlefield, Manchester.
Tel. 0161 8322244 www.mosi.org.uk *Just what a
museum should be!*

THE SCIENCE MUSEUM, London.
Tel. 020 794 24000 www.nmsi.ac.uk *Superb modern
museum, which still has its fine collection of smaller
items on show.*

THE THINK TANK, Millennium Point, Curzon St,
Birmingham. Tel. 0121 202 2222 www.thinktank.ac
Very modern with lots to attract the young.

Bibliography

Neil Cossons   *Industrial Archaeology* (David & Charles)
David Eveleigh   *Candle Lighting* (Shire)
Stirling Everard   *The History of the Gas Light & Coke Co.* (A&C Black)
John Griffiths   *The Third Man* (Andre Deutsch)
Stephen Halliday   *The Great Stink of London* (Sutton)
Christopher Hibbert *The English* (Paladin)
Julie Horan   *The Porcelain God* (Robson Books)
Charles Jacobson   *Ties that Bind* (The University of Pittsburgh Press)
David Kynaston   *Yesterday's Britain* (The Reader's Digest)
Noral Lofts   *Domestic Life in England* (Book Club Associates)
Linda Osband   *Victorian House Styles* (David & Charles)
Valerie Porter   *Yesterday's Countryside* (David & Charles)
Peter Naylor   *Water Supply* (Shire)
Robert Ward   *London's New River* (Historical Publications)
Lawrence Wright   *Clean and Decent* (Routledge & Kegan Paul)

INDEX

Also in the Living History Series

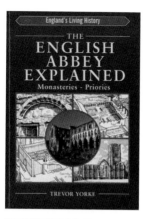
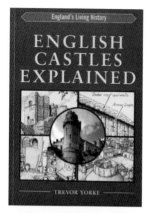

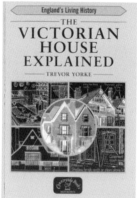
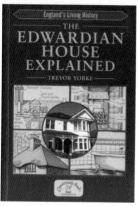

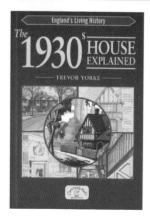
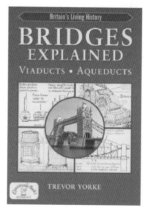

Also in the Living History Series

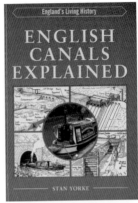
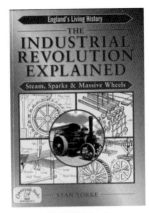
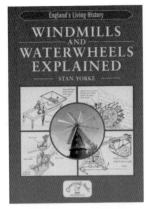

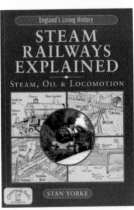

*To view our complete range of books,
please visit us at
www.countrysidebooks.co.uk*